The TRUTH about Employee Engagement

Uncover the Reasons Employees Leave and How to Get Them to Stay

Cheryl R. Bates, DM

ISBN: 978-0-692-19479-9

Published by Cheryl R. Bates

Library of Congress Control Number: 2018911577

Printing 10 9 8 7 6 5 4 3 2 1

The TRUTH about Employee Engagement

Uncover the Reasons Employees Leave and How to Get Them to Stay

Cheryl R. Bates, DM

CONTENTS

ACKNOWLEDGEMENTS

This book would not be possible without the people who trusted me with their innermost thoughts and feelings about their workplace. I value every moment we spent together laughing and sometimes crying. I felt your passion and your desire to be a part of the solution.

It is your voices that drive me as I put pen to paper. It is your faces I see when the going gets tough. It takes courage and determination to share your voice and stand in your truth, even if that truth is contrary to others. I will continue to fight the good fight for and with you. You are my reason.

To my family – Sandra, Alphonso, Cynthia, Latrece, Roy, Nickolas and Jonathan – thank you for your support, encouragement, patience and LOVE. For all the times I've chartered new territories, stepped outside of my comfort zone and dared to live my life's purpose, you cheered me on and was the wind on my back pushing me forward. This was a journey that you shared and I thank you for coming along for the ride. Jasmine, you are the person I see when I think of the little girls who will know they too can realize their dreams and goals. May GOD bless you all and keep you in his loving embrace.

PREFACE

The U.S. workforce is struggling and it appears that many companies are failing in their efforts to stop the bleeding. Either they don't care or they don't know how to stop the mass exodus of people who leave their organizations every day. According to a report by Gallup (2018), 51% of the workforce are looking to leave their employers.

Despite the efforts to recruit great talent, companies find it challenging to engage and retain great people. I have worked for many years with companies trying to "fix" the problem. I propose that companies are looking at this thing the wrong way. *They are using external methods to fix internal problems.*

In the *Truth about Employee Engagement,* I suggest that the strategies and methods used by leaders in U.S. corporations are the main problems. Many leaders place the blame on middle managers, and in some cases employees, for the lack of engagement within their organizations, seldom turning the mirror on themselves. Some leaders take the view of "*If they don't like it here, they can leave.*" And that is exactly what employees are doing, leaving.

The paradigm used by leaders in many U.S. companies needs to change. Many of the methods being used in companies today are decades old. And from my experience, the body of knowledge and methods of practice for employee engagement practitioners is lacking or non-existent. And to make the problem worse, companies continue to turn to outside consulting firms to fix internal problems. Well, I'm fed up with the same old approaches, and it appears that employees are fed up too!

I wrote this book for professionals tasked with employee engagement who are weary of the old-school methods used to address current situations. It is time for employee engagement professionals to create our own unique methods for addressing employee engagement and growing the profession from within our own ranks. That is what I offer in this book. Rather than standing in the background complaining and pointing fingers, it is my responsibility as an employee engagement professional to offer alternative frameworks and methodologies and new practice ideas to grow the body of knowledge and I am proud to offer that in *The Truth about Employee Engagement.*

My hope is that employee engagement professionals, those working within companies, those who interact daily with the organization's people and those whose passion is helping employees love their jobs and workplaces step up. I ask that you join me by adding new methods and frameworks that offer our profession additional ways of addressing why employees leave and why they stay and methods for facilitating employee happiness at work.

If you are passionate about changing the U.S. work environment through employee engagement practices and you are looking for new and creative ways to approach the business of employee engagement, this book is for you.

CHAPTER 1

THE EMPLOYEE ENGAGEMENT ENIGMA

To win in the marketplace you must first win in the workplace
- Doug Conant

Employee engagement has long been touted as the key to a happy and loyal workforce. Uncover what it takes to make an employee happy, and you're guaranteed a productive and committed workforce leading to greater financial outcomes for the organization. If this is true, why are 70% of U.S. workers disengaged at work (Gallup, 2017) and 51% actively seeking other employment (Gallup, 2018)? More than half of the U.S. workforce is looking for ways to close the door on their current employers.

Employee engagement, a term coined and made popular by the Gallup Organization, is described as a "measurable degree of an employee's positive or negative emotional attachment to their job, colleagues and organization which profoundly influences their willingness to learn and perform at work" (Davis, 2017). However, there is a myriad of definitions in the literature for the construct including the following.

- *Employee engagement is "the individual's involvement and satisfaction with as well as enthusiasm for work" (Harter, Schmidt and Hayes, 2002).*
- *The illusive force that motivates employees to higher levels of performance. This coveted energy is similar to commitment to the organization, job ownership and pride, more discretionary effort (time and energy), passion and excitement, commitment to execution and the bottom line. (Wellins & Concelman, 2004).*
- *Feelings and attitudes employees have toward their jobs and organizations (Wellins & Concelman, 2004).*
- *A positive attitude held by the employee towards the organization and its values. An engaged employee is aware of the*

> *business context, works with colleagues to improve performance within the job for the benefit of the organization. The organization must develop and nurture engagement, which is a two-way relationship between employer and employee. (Robinson, Perryman & Hayday, 2004).*

There are many definitions of the employee engagement construct, each one carrying its own subtleties. It is important for an organization to agree upon the construct that best describes their intent and desired outcomes for improving its workplace. Agreement ensures that everyone in the organization is moving in the same direction as it relates to their understanding of the employee engagement construct.

Employee engagement has been shown to have a statistical relationship with productivity, profitability, employee retention, safety, and customer satisfaction (Buckingham & Coffman, 1999; Coffman & Gonzalez-Molina, 2002). Many companies operate under the assumption that if an employee is engaged at work, turnover reduces, productivity increases, quality and safety improve and financial outcomes are enhanced. When an employee is not engaged at work, as is the case in the U.S., what are the potential outcomes? Now here is where it gets interesting.

If an employee is engaged at work, can we assume that he or she is bringing their best selves to the workplace and what does that look like? Can we agree that if one brings their best selves to work, they are more likely to produce great work products, deliver exceptional customer service and contribute to quality and safety in the workplace? If true, can we agree that the work outcomes in the U.S. could be substandard at best if we believe Gallup that 70% of the U.S. workforce is not engaged?

Think about what this means for the U.S. and the delivery of products and services. Let's take it a step further. How does this look for the employees of a hospital – nurses, hospitalists, physical therapists, dietitians, housekeeping, nursing assistants, etc.? The next time you are in your physician's office or have a loved one hospitalized, look around. Would you be satisfied that seven out of 10 of those healthcare workers may not be giving their best as they care for you or your loved one? Or, should you just hope and pray that the three engaged employees at work that day are assigned to your case?

In an employee engagement and commitment guide written for the Society for Human Resource Management (SHRM), Vance (2006) wrote, "The greater an employee's engagement, the more likely he or she is to 'go the extra mile' and deliver excellent on-the-job performance. In addition, engaged employees may be more likely to commit to staying with their current organization." However, employee engagement continues to be an enigma for many companies. No matter how committed to building better workplaces, knowing where to start and how to stop the bleeding continues to elude many companies.

Why do companies continue to struggle with unhappy employees that drive up turnover costs as they slam the door behind them trading up for what they believe will be greener pastures? Interestingly, many companies that experience higher employee engagement scores continue to experience employee turnover, low productivity, poor quality and decreased safety, leaving leaders scratching their heads and wondering what is happening? What they may not understand is that engagement, or what appears to be engagement, does not always equal a happy employee willing to give more of their discretionary effort to the company. Many employees come to work every day seemingly engaged, productive (on paper) and unhappy.

Employee engagement consultants would have you believe that if an employee is not engaged, they will underperform. This is not always true. I know this because I was one of those seemingly engaged employees turning out exceptional work results, and very few people knew. While productive, I was unhappy and I was not alone. Many other people were in the same boat. My colleagues and I spoke often about the realities we were experiencing in our workplace. We were intrinsically motivated to deliver exceptional results, but inside we were empty and numb to the organization.

My leaders saw me as a dedicated, happy and engaged employee because that is what I wanted them to see. I consistently received "exceeds expectations" on annual performance reviews and going above and beyond was routine for me. But while seemingly engaged, I was extremely unhappy. I came to work every day intrinsically motivated to make a difference, not because of my dedication to the company, but because I was driven internally by the need to succeed. I went through the day smiling and ducking into any corner I could to get away from unworthy leaders, routine and boring work and the lack of positive recognition. When I left the job each day, I was drained and miserable.

By all accounts, I was a disengaged employee, but on paper and business results, I showed up as engaged. I knew that something was wrong with the theory and concepts around employee engagement. What were leaders missing and why were they not trying to understand others like me who appeared engaged on paper but in reality, were disengaged and undercover? How much more could a person like me bring to the workplace if I were truly engaged? And, I often wondered how could I contribute to a body of knowledge that would help leaders jerk the cover off pretenders like me and really engage them?

I wrote previously that I am intrinsically motivated to succeed, so with that energy, I offer this body of knowledge that I pray will be read by leaders who wish to learn more about diving deeper into the psyche of employees to really understand what it means to be an engaged employee. Living by the annual employee survey results will not get you there – we must learn to supplement these surveys with our own analyses throughout the year that will add value to existing methods and get us closer to the TRUTH!

I hypothesize that companies will experience greater workplaces if leaders dive deeper. And, dare I say, relying on external consulting firms to learn about your employees is not proving to be the most effective way to understand and KNOW your employees. And, it's certainly not helping companies move the needle in the right direction!

Employee engagement consulting firms would have you believe that they have the answers, if only you hire them to solve the inherent problems? Is this true, and if so, where is the proof of improvement? If studies show that employee satisfaction and engagement continue to decline in the U.S., how have consultants and other firms contributed to the lack of employee loyalty and unhappy workplaces?

I hypothesize that it may be their approach to the problem. And, I suggest that companies are not taking responsibility for understanding their own organizations from the inside, but instead relying on external consultants that have little to no personal experience in that company's culture and everyday work environment.

Organizations often depend on employee surveys and other quantitative and qualitative tools (e.g., spot surveys, culture surveys) to help them understand their workplace dynamics. The problem is that organizations often turn to the same group of firms and organizations that tout themselves as having the best surveys and tools that will surely provide insight and strategies for improvement.

There is a myriad of consulting tools, and fees that come along with them, promising to help you understand your people problems, improve retention and be recognized as one of the better places to work. The cycle is obvious and is repeated year after year by companies who have bought into the process of surveying every year, meeting to discuss the results, implementing a few programs and applying for recognition awards – all to no avail. Employees remain disconnected, disengaged and miserable.

The question becomes, is this cycle a process that garners results or is it a check the box activity to which companies subscribe and use to impress their boards and annoy their employees? I can tell you that employees are on to it and that is why they hate the sight of the yearly marketing emails, flyers and promotions announcing "Let Your Voice be Heard." I know this firsthand as I was responsible for these announcements and marketing tools and employees would tell me to my face why they did not believe in the survey process. I knew it was a fraud! I too did not believe in the process and knew there had to be a better way!

When I suggested changes to the process using new methods and frameworks, brick walls were put up by leaders – no time, no budget, not interested. So, the cycle continued. Unfortunately, some leaders are heavily invested into believing that knowledge can only be generated and purchased from consulting firms, often neglecting the potential of their own internal knowledge creators.

Little and Little (2006) suggested that companies that measure their employees' level of engagement with the assumption that engagement leads to increased outcomes continue to research the construct to "better understand what they are measuring and predicting." In this book, I attempt to do just that, examine the usage of surveys historically and their impact on employee engagement, loyalty and organizational culture, and offer a new framework and methodology for the continued measurement of engagement and organizational culture. In addition, I hypothesize that if you partner with your employees and include them in the process, change can happen from within.

It is a fact that many organizations continue to struggle with the employee engagement construct and I offer reasons for this phenomenon. Once we understand the impact, which in many cases has not resulted in happy, engaged employees, I offer a solution, a succinct framework and methodology to enable organizations to take control of their own employee engagement destiny. I have used this framework and method in my employee engagement practices and the results have been phenomenal.

While many companies focus wholly on the workforce (i.e., front-line employees), there needs to be a focused and holistic approach to study the whole organization that uncovers the real culprit of disengaged employees and leaders and weak workplace culture. That's right, a holistic and systemic approach to employee engagement that focuses on all people in the organization throughout the employment hierarchy, including senior leaders and executives.

Another goal of this book is to introduce the need for a focused and deliberate body of practice for employee engagement professionals. Much of the work in employee engagement is conducted by practitioners from human resource professions. The practice of creating, implementing and measuring employee engagement programs is often tasked to those whose primary jobs are employee relations, labor relations, learning and development, and in some organizations, organizational development. I contend that this contributes to a loose and unfocused practice of employee engagement and further disengages employees.

The critical and complex work of rallying the workforce, helping people love their jobs and the companies for which they work and creating great work environments is often conducted by people whose expertise lies elsewhere. Therefore, the practice of employee engagement is anything but a focused body of professional practice. It is often a secondary part of a person's job – many times attached to a job description as "other duties as identified." In these situations, expecting stellar results and improved work environments becomes a bad nightmare for both the employee and the company, from which leaders and employees are struggling to awake. And we wonder why people are unhappy at work?

Employees are smarter than we think - they see the secondary position attached to their wellbeing and they respond with low productivity, poor quality, reduced safety, absenteeism and turnover. I have had employees tell me that employee engagement is a joke. If the overall employee experience and programs are treated as "add-ons" to someone's job description and viewed and approached as secondary, why do we expect first-rate results with second-rate methods? One can see how this sets up a disastrous situation for all involved. This book provides insight into the value and contribution a dedicated employee engagement (EE) practitioner can add that ultimately translates to a company's value proposition – happy employees and a great bottom line.

The phenomenon of "other duties as assigned" is interesting. I suggest that the additional duties category on the job description is a result of what work life in U.S. corporations has become. I call it the "RIF Life." Layoffs and downsizing are categorized as reductions in force (RIF).

If you have worked for companies in the U.S., you probably have experienced "RIF Life." It is likely that you, a family member or friend have been laid off from their job in a U.S. company. I believe it is a great contributor to why many U.S. workers are unhappy at work and appear disloyal to companies.

How can leaders expect loyalty when employees continue to experience layoffs? How can employees give their best when they come to work every day fearing the next RIF? Given our country's history, their fears are realistic. Today, the "Rif Life" continues to negatively impact employee engagement in this country and employees continue to appear disloyal to leaders when they leave or quit the company – before the company quits them (i.e., RIFs).

In *The Disposable American,* Uchitelle (2006) traces the rise of job security from the 1950s to the decline of job security arriving with the onset of laying off American workers in the 1970s with the advent of global competition. Uchitelle suggests that the phenomenon of laying off American workers has resulted in a loss of job security and work dignity. He goes on to discuss the trauma that being laid off inflicts on the American people and their overall mental health that is sure to undermine productivity and happiness at work. The bleeding has not stopped as U.S. companies continue to use layoffs as a strategic imperative for financial success and the U.S. workforce continues to tremble at work in fear of the next layoff.

There seems to be an inherent contradiction between a company's use of layoffs as an economic strategy and their desire to increase employee engagement and improve work environments. One has only to read the daily news to see which company is laying off employees to make up for profit loss. There is ample research that proves that layoffs are counterproductive to employee engagement.

In a study by Murphy (2015), it was found that after a layoff, employees unaffected do not work harder. In fact, 74% of surviving employees say their productivity declined and 69% of employees remaining after a layoff say that their product or service declined after the layoff.

Findings from Murphy (2015) on the state of the workplace after company layoffs include the following.

- **87%** of surviving workers say they are **less likely to recommend** their organization as a good place to work.
- **64%** of surviving workers say the **productivity** of their colleagues has also **declined**.
- **81%** of surviving workers say the **service** that customers receive has **declined**.
- **77%** of surviving workers say they see **more errors** and mistakes being made.
- **61%** of surviving workers say they believe their company's future **prospects** are **worse**.

And we wonder why our workforce appears disloyal, disengaged and dissatisfied with U.S. companies? As with any trauma, and being laid off is certainly a trauma, healing is necessary. However, how many companies are focused on healing their employees following a layoff? Could it be that the focus on healing would be too extensive and expensive due to repeated layoffs being a business imperative?

As an EE practitioner, I have often heard employees talk about the fear of being laid off. I have been a part of and witness to the process of what companies call a reduction in force. They are brutal and demoralizing, and not just for the unfortunate people losing their jobs, but for those who remain. There is a level of grief in getting laid off and even for those who remain behind and, unfortunately, many leaders are clueless and expect business as usual when the desk next to yours is now empty and your work friend is gone and out of a job. The relationships made at work are major contributors to happiness at work (Riordan, 2013) and when that relationship is severed through a layoff, the effect(s) can be devastating (Uchitelle, 2006).

Murphy (2015) calls this phenomenon "layoff survival stress," adding that "there is a myth that surviving employees will be so grateful that they still have a job that they will work harder and be more productive." As this study shows, the opposite is usually true. And we expect our employees to be good little boys and girls and return to work as if nothing ever happened. And, let us not forget the additional work, often without additional pay, these "left behind" employees are expected to absorb following the RIFs, which adds another whole level of trauma.

To illustrate my point, read the memo from MIT's human resources (MIT, HR, 2009) that provides guidance to leaders whose staff were affected by layoffs.

> *"Your ability to communicate effectively and regularly with your staff after the layoffs will prove invaluable in the long term. People may show signs of anxiety, lack of commitment, and even a decrease in productivity and creativity. In the weeks and months that follow a layoff or reorganization, strong leadership strategies are required to help employees focus on the priorities at hand and to recommit themselves to the organization. In companies where there have been layoffs, fear can undermine daily work and lead to loss of productivity. There may be gossip, rumors, and lots of lost time. People may begin to see colleagues as competitors, eroding the collegiality and spirit in your group."*

While the information on what employees may experience is on point, where is the compassion and commitment from the company leadership to its remaining employees? For the company, it's business as usual, and dare I say employees are instructed to keep their heads up and remain engaged and "recommit to the company." Are they serious?

Think about the managers and supervisors that must rally the troops. Where is the empathy and compassion for these people who must now practice industrial psychology, a practice for which they are surely ill qualified? They are instructed to quickly get back to business as usual, putting their grief and emotions aside?

How can we rationalize the desire to improve employees' happiness at work if U.S. companies continue to use layoffs as a strategic imperative and expect those left behind to carry on as usual? Keep in mind that this type of guidance and language is standard practice in U.S. companies.

Improving employee engagement is in the hands of the leaders of U.S. companies. They can turn this around and change the employee experience and improve employee engagement, but it will take a change in the damaging practices leaders continuously use to improve their financial bottom lines. I do not agree that it is employee engagement and loyalty vs. the bottom line. This is a dangerous assumption and practice and one that should be removed from strategy consideration, that is if companies are honestly focused on improving employee engagement.

CHAPTER 2

DEBUNKING EMPLOYEE ENGAGEMENT MYTHS

Myth: Employee engagement programs lead to improved workforce environments and best places to work.

Each year, companies are recognized for being better places to work by organizations such as Fortune, Modern Healthcare, Top 100 Best Places to Work and the list goes on. If we can believe the lists published each year that suggest work environments are improving, what are we to believe about engagement? How can a work environment improve and engagement remain poor (Gallup, 2017)? Shouldn't there be a positive correlation that tells us that when work environments improve so does employee engagement? If that is true, why is employee engagement continuing to show up poorly in the U.S.?

How do we begin to reconcile the obvious employee engagement lies and gaps? That is the purpose of this book, to help leaders and EE practitioners understand the complex components of employee engagement and the differences between creating what organizations believe to be better work environments and actually creating environments where people are actually engaged and in alignment with the organization and its purpose.

Myth: When employees are happy and engaged, turnover decreases.

If this statement is true, why is employee turnover continuing to rise (Catalyst, 2016)? Turnover data for specific companies can be difficult to obtain for obvious reasons. Who wants to publicize the mass exodus of their people? In a company for which I worked, employee engagement scores for overall satisfaction were consistently between 70% and 73% (out of 100%) for several years. Compared to other companies in the database of the external survey company we employed, that was not a poor engagement score for a company. Benchmarks of other companies overall were rarely above 76% during the same time period.

This is where I differ in my opinion with the methods used, that is comparing one's company with benchmarks. This practice is adhered to like a bible in many companies. The first question asked by my leaders when employee survey results were distributed was, "What is the benchmark?" If the benchmark was at or below their score, this was cause for celebration or at least a sigh of relief. If the benchmark was higher, heads hung low. I would often ask why the benchmark was such an important piece of information, especially when the benchmark scores were not stellar?

If the rating scale is between 1 and 100, why are scores that would get you no better than a C in school acceptable and cause for celebration? The bigger question is if engagement is continuing to decline in the U.S., are we using effective measures and strategies for engagement? Is there a better way to move the needle? I say, "Yes," and that is the premise of this book – to arm leaders and EE practitioners with an alternative to old-school methods for addressing employee engagement and experience, or at the very least, better understand the gaps and why employees are heading for the door with smoke at their heels.

Myth: Surveying employees annually will increase employee engagement, the employee experience and overall employee satisfaction.

Many employee engagement consulting firms recommend that U.S. companies survey their employees annually. According to Harris (2016) of Quantum Workplace, companies experience better engagement when surveying annually versus every other year. If true, why do employees in the U.S. continue to express dissatisfaction and report low engagement with their employers (Gallup, 2017)? And, why do employees continuously express frustration when the annual surveys are announced, and why are many employees reluctant to even participate?

While leading the employee survey process for one of the largest companies in the U.S., I would often hear expressions of dissatisfaction with the survey experience from both leaders and employees. Leaders did not want to promote the survey and employees certainly didn't want to participate. I was often asked if their responses would truly be anonymous and if they expressed their true opinion(s) would their name follow their response(s)? Why would they ask this if all was good? Why would an employee want to be incognito if they were happy with the company and their work experiences?

In my experience with companies for which I worked, we used external companies and the data and results were stored on their external server. But again, that depends on how a company approaches their survey process. Some use internal staff and internal servers. In these situations, anonymity and confidentiality could easily be compromised.

I constantly experienced high levels of anxiety and frustrations from employees who felt obligated and pressured to complete the survey, and I was often told that they did not express their true feelings because of fear of retaliation. I experienced much difficulty convincing people that their responses would not be directly tied back to them but instead reported in aggregate. I truly believe that their fear and daily experiences would not allow them to believe what I told them about the process. So, what does this mean for the validity of the employee survey results?

Promoting the annual survey is a major part of the annual employee survey process. Many companies go all out to create awareness of the upcoming survey, using a variety of marketing and communication tools to gain interest and participation. I was heavily involved in creating such awareness. We developed targeted communication toolkits that included newsletter articles, social media tools, fun activities, swag, videos and other innovative methods to create excitement. We encouraged employees to have their voices heard and don't be left out because we cared about how they felt about their workplace.

Many days, I felt that I was the only person excited about the upcoming survey. I was passionate about and truly believed in employee engagement. There were days where I had to pump myself up and put on a smiling face, knowing that I believed there was a much better way to excite people about loving what they do and where they work.

I often felt conflicted with the direction of the company's engagement strategy and believed that this annual pony show was not best for learning about their "best asset," their people. Many days I felt this was a crock of you know what – a well-used cliché that sounded mediocre at best. And employees knew it! Employees show their discontent with companies every year by screaming,

"We're Not Happy!" And the continuing decline in employee engagement results in the U.S. proves it.

It is evident that there is a problem in this country when it comes to people loving, or at least having a positive affinity for their jobs and the companies for which they work. I contend that the problem lies in the approach to creating better work environments including the use of RIFs as a strategic imperative.

In my experience, many EE practitioners' primary focus is on social programs in their efforts to positively impact engagement. Give enough parties and picnics and voila, our workforce is happy and engaged. Not so much.

I contend that employee engagement and the overall employee experience cannot be built solely with social programs. Improving the work life of employees is so much more and much more complex. Today's EE practitioner must be steeped in a systematic method for improving the workplace and the work environment. No more social coordinators and no more party planners. Improving the overall employee experience demands more.

I am not saying there is not a place in the overall program for these activities, but to effectively move the needle on creating an engaged workforce, we need EE practitioners steeped in a methodology that can impact change, not just put on great parties and picnics. And, we need informed leaders to support this critical body of practice. So, what do we do? How do we turn this around? How do we really determine what makes our people happy and improves the workplace?

If it is true that engaged employees and great work environments lead to improved productivity, better quality, improved safety and greater financial success for companies in the U.S., isn't it worth taking a critical look at the way we approach employee engagement and the livid experiences of employees in the U.S.?

That is the purpose of this book – to provide a methodology and framework for EE practitioners to better understand the gaps in the employee's overall experience that is leading to unhappiness at work, low productivity and mass exodus. And let us not forget about the "RIF Life," the use of layoffs and reductions in force and their contribution to disengagement.

CHAPTER 3

THE CASE FOR EMPLOYEE ENGAGEMENT PRACTITIONERS

In the previous chapter, I introduced the notion of having a focused body of practice and EE practitioners charged with creating programs and initiatives that positively impact work environments and the employee experience. In this chapter, I suggest the knowledge, skills and abilities for consideration that could set this profession and practitioner up for success.

I also propose that employee engagement should be a recognized profession with the likes of human resources, employee relations, organizational development, learning and development, compensation, benefits and labor relations. I think you get my point.

First, organizational leaders need to be on board and agree that EE practitioners are critical to improving work environments and as such employee engagement should be a stand-alone profession and occupation – not the traditional "add-on" status currently employed by many organizations.

While there appear to be a few companies moving in this direction, there are not enough focused practitioners to move the needle on employee engagement in this country and as long as organizations treat the profession as a secondary job or set of activities, employee engagement will continue to suffer. It's like the old saying, if you keep doing what you've done, you will keep getting what you got. In other words, nothing will change, at least not significantly.

Knowledge, Skills, and Abilities (KSAs)

Historically, those tasked with employee engagement have mainly been human resource professionals. While there may be others that have been tasked with employee engagement, let's look at the human resources professional category as it is the one most frequently assigned to employee engagement, employee surveys and resulting action planning.

In many U.S. companies, traditional functions of human resources professionals include benefits administration, total reward programs, compensation, new hire onboarding, recruiting, policy, compliance, employee relations, human resource information systems, labor relations, diversity, inclusion, learning and development and workplace safety.

While having human resource experience and skills are beneficial, an EE practitioner may have a better chance at success if they have experience and skills in a myriad of occupations including some that are not from the traditional human resources field.

For example, in addition to having experience in human resources functions, a background in communications, marketing, research and employment law could prove beneficial. I am not advocating for EE practitioners occupying multiple workspaces and continuums, only that having the background experience in a variety of functions could prove beneficial.

Recently, I came across a great example of the current situation when it comes to hiring employee engagement professionals. I perused a job advertisement for a Director of Employee Engagement. I was immediately excited! Finally, I am seeing more organizations identify engagement as a professional practice. I was quickly disappointed. The job description was all over the place. This person would be responsible for recruiting, new hire onboarding, benefits administration and several other tasks. "What is this?" I thought.

How can a person succeed with so many varied responsibilities and what does this job have to do with engaging the organization's people and improving their work experiences? And, how was this position benchmarked to determine a fair and accurate pay range?

This example proves my point. We need to identify specific areas of practice and determine standards of practice for employee engagement professionals. What we have now is a hodgepodge of tasks strung together that do not set people up for success and do not set the profession apart.

A variety of skills and experiences have been extremely helpful in my practice of employee engagement. I have had to develop communication tools (i.e., newsletters, social media posts, video, etc.) to create awareness of activities, events and initiatives and creatively market them to employees and leaders. I've also used knowledge obtained in paralegal studies to determine next steps for action when I've learned of discrepancies and violations in ethics, compliance and policy.

In addition, my knowledge, skills and abilities (KSAs) obtained from more than 15 years of human resources experience have been instrumental in helping leaders build actions plans that improved the overall work experience including employee capabilities, succession planning, benefits, total rewards, work environments, work/life balance, career paths, new hire onboarding, diversity and inclusion and many other areas identified as needing improvement to create a better place to work.

Organizations should think hard and long to ensure clarity before establishing job descriptions. When developing an EE practitioner job description, knowledge about the profession's standard of practice should be well thought out. The core competencies for an EE practitioner may overlap in skill set with not only human resources, but those from other professions. For example, a list of core competencies for the EE practitioner *could include some* of the following KSAs (in alphabetical order).

- Budget management
- Communications (written and verbal)
- Conducting needs assessments
- Culture building
- Customer service
- Employee relations
- Employee survey management, administration and action planning
- Employment law
- Focus group facilitation: The ability to conduct focus groups is usually honed in professions such as marketing, advertising and public relations – none of which are traditional human resource activities.
- Labor relations
- Learning and development
- Managing and coordinating special events
- Marketing
- Organizational development (OD)
- Qualitative and quantitative design and analyses
- Public relations
- Public speaking
- Relationship and team building

- Research and analytics
- Strategic planning

Organizations should think strategically when creating job descriptions and core competencies for EE practitioners. To improve the chances for success and to avoid a potentially frustrated professional, look for a well-rounded person with KSAs that cut across several professions including human resources. While there is some overlap in the KSAs needed for human resources, marketers, OD, employee engagement and others, the methods and approach for EE practitioners differ. The difference is the methodology and framework from which EE practitioners should work. That is the purpose for creating the framework and methodology proposed in this book.

Being an EE practitioner is not easy. You will find that oftentimes you are in the middle of employees and leaders with your arms outstretched and each group is pulling you in a different direction. On days that I have not felt this way, I didn't feel I was doing my job.

I have found that there is an inherent conflict between employees and leaders, many times unrealistically present.

It is our jobs as practitioners to uncover the root causes and create awareness of the conflict or gaps in perception and expectations and help leaders and employees close these gaps. EE practitioners should be described as organizational diagnosticians working to detect abnormalities in the system and offering a course of treatment for improvement.

I propose that the following definition frame the profession.

> *The function of employee engagement practitioners should be to uncover the root causes of disengagement and create awareness of the conflict or gaps in perception and expectations and help executives and employees close these gaps. EE practitioners should be described as organizational diagnosticians working to detect abnormalities in the system and offering a course of treatment for improvement.*

Did you notice that party and event planning did not make the cut? That is on purpose!

CHAPTER 4

THE BATES FRAMEWORK AND METHODOLOGY FOR EMPLOYEE ENGAGEMENT PRACTITIONERS

Theoretical Framework

Theoretical frameworks are ways of looking at the social world. They provide collections of assumptions, concepts and forms of explanations (Neuman, 2003). In this case, the social world is comprised of people within an organization. The framework proposed in this book, The Bates Employee Experience Framework (BEEF, Figure 4.1), is one I created, tested and implemented in my work as an EE practitioner.

THE BATES EMPLOYEE EXPERIENCE FRAMEWORK (BEEF)

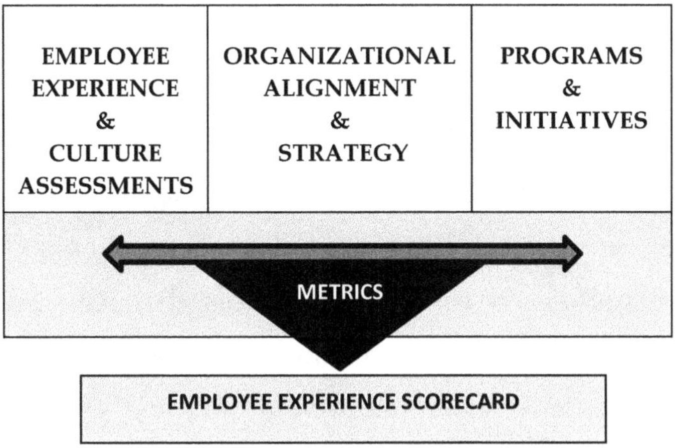

Figure 4.1. The BATES Employee Experience Framework (BEEF)

The BEEF framework provides EE practitioners with methods to use in their day-to-day work activities. The framework contains five components.

1. Engagement and culture assessments to determine baseline data that will inform your approach and strategies upon which to build program(s)

2. Methods for strategy alignment
3. Program and initiative development
4. Metrics and measurements
5. The Employee Experience Scorecard

I believe that the BATES Employee Experience Framework provides the necessary components an EE practitioner needs to critically assess the organization's people (all people), culture and workplace to positively impact work environments, culture and the overall employee experience. The framework is transferable and can be used in a myriad of organizations in the U.S. and abroad.

Methodology

The BATES Engagement and Culture Assessments (BECA) form the framework's anchor and inform the method. The assessments are diagnostic tools used to provide the methodology for capturing baseline information from which to build employee engagement programs, initiatives and activities within an organization.

The Employee Experience Feedback and Culture Assessments determines baseline and will help you tell your organization's current story. The assessment is critical to understanding the organization's current situation and getting into the minds and hearts of all employees, including senior leaders.

The assessment stage is the most critical process in the framework. Getting it right will determine the success, or failure, of the entire employee engagement program. In other words, your employees may continue to head for the nearest exit if their story is inaccurately told and lacks empathy.

So, take your time and be thoughtful and mindful as you capture and analyze the results. Your results will tell a story that contains all of the elements you need to move forward in creating an amazing and effective employee engagement program. The assessments are discussed later in detail in Chapter 5.

The framework's second component is infrastructure and strategy alignment. One of the mistakes practitioners make in employee engagement work is the lack of alignment with company strategy and infrastructure. Practitioners jump head first into program and initiative development without giving much thought to why they are doing what they do. I propose that this is due to a lack of a guiding framework and methodology for the practice of employee engagement. I have been there and done that.

When I first began working in employee engagement, I was handed a list of tasks – manage the employee survey, help HR leaders develop action plans, develop reports, analyze data, help leaders understand their results, help leaders develop action plans for improvement, build recognition programs and on and on. Nowhere was there a rhyme or reason for why I was doing that for which I was tasked. Nor was there a tie to overall company strategy, infrastructure or accountability.

I often felt lost and on an island. If you are like me, I need a reason why or it all becomes one big passionless blur. I operated in this blur for quite some time while trying to find an anchor for the job I was performing. When I could not, I knew I had to create my own anchor, framework and methodology for what I was doing and make it make sense to those for whom I was working.

It became my goal to provide clarity for the EE practitioner, removing that blur that many times rendered me passionless and disengaged. And that is why I'm writing this book, to remove the blur and provide practitioners with a guiding framework and methodology to effectively and professionally practice the craft that is so critical to employee engagement.

Organizations typically tie their people strategies into overall HR strategies. If this is your case, work with your HR leader to ensure alignment with the company's people goals. A few questions to ask yourself include the following. Once you are comfortable with your response, discuss the topics with your HR team.

- How can what I do as an EE practitioner tie into and align with company and HR strategy?
- How can my work influence employee turnover?
- How can employee engagement be used as a tool to enhance the overall employee experience?
- How can we engage and partner with leaders in improving the overall work experience?
- How do we ensure accountability for engagement?
- How do you track and measure success?
- What measurements and metrics should we consider?

Infrastructure is critical to the EE practitioner's success. In addition to what you may be tasked with, how will you get it done? How can you set yourself up for success? Are the goals for employee engagement attainable with the number of staff and resources allotted to you? These questions are critical and many practitioners overlook these considerations when their goals are agreed upon.

In many organizations, the EE practitioner is often a department of one but is expected to address engagement issues for the entire organization. This expectation is unrealistic. Raising your hand for more resources, budget or people should be at the beginning of your work, not when you've missed expectations.

Set yourself up for success by assessing what needs to be done based on your baseline assessments. Obtain agreement for how you are to move forward with the resources you have available to you. Do not hesitate to push back when expectations do not align with your resources. Remember, that you will be held accountable for what you have agreed to up front.

The third component of the framework includes programs and initiatives, which should be based on information gleaned from the engagement and culture assessments, the diagnostic part of your work. Once the EE practitioner conducts and analyzes the baseline assessments, evidence will arise that lead to programs and initiatives needed to affect change. Remember to assess your infrastructure before you agree to goals and initiatives. Can you be successful with the resources are allotted to you?

Providing the foundation for the framework are metrics and the Employee Experience Scorecard. It is often said that if it cannot be measured, it doesn't exist. Well, we know that "it" exists, it just needs a succinct method for assessment tracking and measurement.

Once you determine your baseline and resulting programs and initiatives, you now need to determine what success looks like for each program and initiative and how each will be measured – all in alignment with the company's strategies, goals and infrastructure. These will become your metrics. Measuring progress against your program goals is critical, and so is having a scorecard that tracks progress and success.

As an example, let's say that you determine that your organization needs a recognition program in order to move the needle on employee engagement and satisfaction and you develop a peer to peer recognition program based on the intelligence gleaned from your baseline assessments. How and when will you know you are successful? This information will inform your metrics.

Metrics are discussed in depth in Chapter 6 where I provide examples of metrics and ways you can potentially measure them. Of course, measurements of success will be identified by you and your leadership team. My goal here is to guide you by providing ideas you can use to determine what best works for your company.

The Employee Experience Scorecard is a relatively new concept to the practice of employee engagement. I have never seen one in practice as a stand-alone component. What I have seen is one measure of overall engagement usually attached to the organization's overall scorecard. That is if the organization believes that measuring employee satisfaction and engagement is important. Unfortunately, many do not.

If we want to be taken seriously as EE practitioners, we must not only develop our own scorecards but also link our programs, initiatives and measurements to the overall business scorecard.

In Chapter 7, I offer suggestions and examples of how to build a simple scorecard that links to the company's deliverables. I suggest using a simple scorecard to start so that the focus can be on identifying and tracking outcomes. Once you have advanced in the framework and methodology offered in this book, you can move to a more sophisticated scorecard. But for now, keep it simple.

CHAPTER 5

THE BECA METHOD

The BATES Engagement and Culture Assessment Model

(BECA)

The BATES Engagement and Culture Assessment Model (BECA Method)

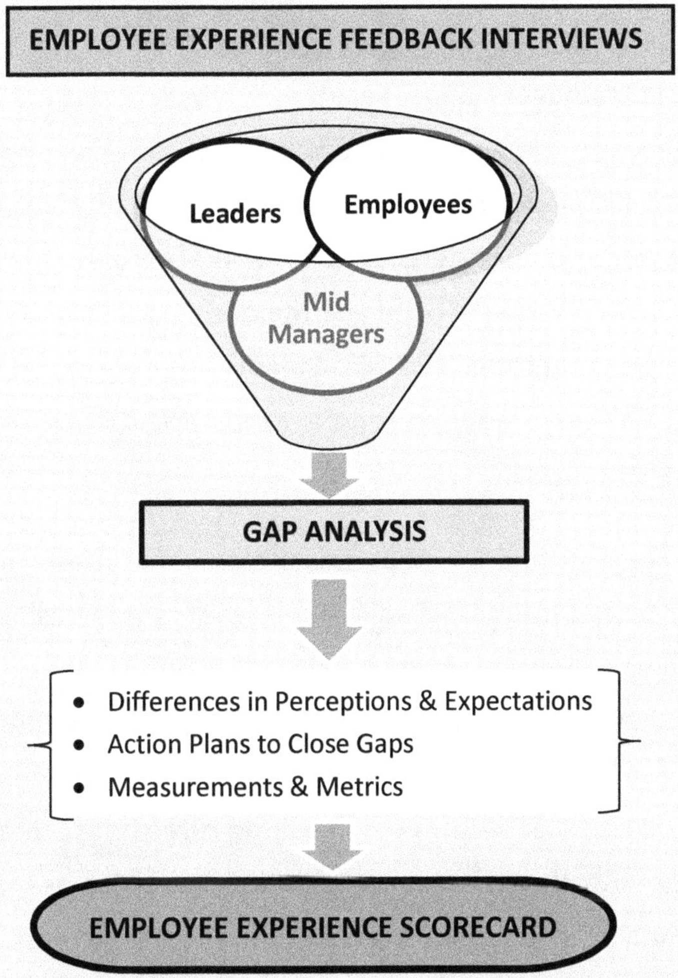

Figure 5.1. The BECA MODEL

The Bates Employee Engagement and Culture Assessment Model (BECA Method) takes it shape from historical employee survey methodology using similar methods such as interviewing and surveying employees, middle managers and executive leaders. It differs in its approach in the way the information is gathered and used to affect change in organizations. While many employee surveys are administered using a solitary method, usually in an online format, the BECA Method is administered in a focus group setting. The assessments are both quantitative and qualitative and provide a forum for discussion in a group setting.

The information that this process has been able to uncover is astounding and many leaders have asked me, "How did you get them to share that information?" One would be surprised at how much an employee will tell you if you just talk to them – not at them. That is what this methodology is built upon, speaking directly to the people and giving them a chance to interact and be heard in a humanistic setting, not from behind a faceless computer or in a solitary room with computers.

The BECA Method differs in another way that is critical to the successful collection of information that will drive programs, initiatives and positive change. The assessments are administered to three groups – employees, middle managers and executive leaders, with the goal of identifying gaps in perceptions and expectations about their specific thoughts around employee engagement and work experiences. From these assessments, a gap analysis is developed. The gap analysis is the key to the methodology. From the gap analysis, one can see the differences in perceptions and expectations among the three groups. That is where you find the gold – in the differences in perceptions and expectations.

The BECA Method has been proven reliable and valid through repeated use and validation in the healthcare and financial services fields. Validity is the degree to which an instrument measures the construct or behavior being assessed. Reliability is the level of consistency obtained when using the instrument (Creswell, 2005).

Validity and reliability were initially tested using a sample of 350 healthcare employees including executive leaders and has since been used with more than 2,500 employees and executive leaders in the healthcare field from a myriad of healthcare professionals (e.g., nurses, clinical technicians, maintenance workers, nursing assistants, food service workers, nurse managers, hospital leaders, etc.). The tool has proven to provide in-depth information needed to affect positive change in employee engagement and organizational culture.

Using the BECA Method, I have been able to gather root cause information that traditional employee surveys typically cannot or do not provide. If one were to employ a firm to do this type of work, the cost would be astronomical and probably still would not yield the results that I have obtained. However, an EE practitioner armed with this framework and methodology can move mountains at a fraction of the cost.

The BECA Method

The BECA Method provides a simple and cost-effective way for EE practitioners to diagnose and offer solutions to improve workplace engagement and culture. The method contains four components that will lead you to improved engagement and work environments in your company.

In this chapter, I will take you step-by-step through each component so that you can immediately begin using the method to discover gaps in the workplace that may be contributing to unhappy employees and toxic work environments. The four components include the following.

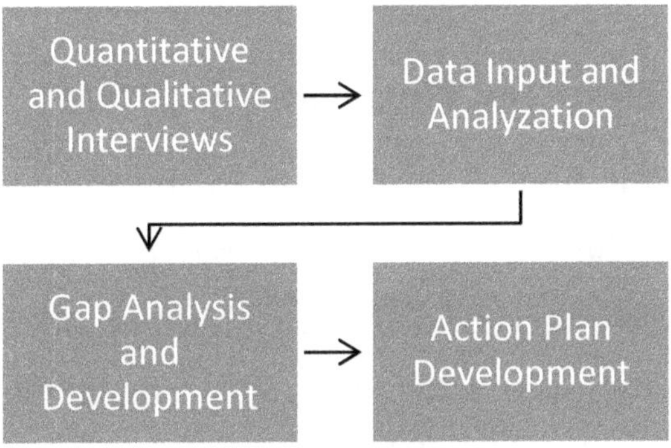

Figure 5.2. BECA Method Components

The discovery of gaps in perception and expectations between all levels of the employment hierarchy is the first step to employee engagement improvement. Discovering gaps in engagement and expectations is the critical component many external firms miss in their work with organizations. This is the core of the BECA Method. The method provides a roadmap for EE practitioners and can ease frustrations about where to start and what to do to improve and add value to the work environment and overall employee happiness and satisfaction.

For your convenience, I have included a BECA Method Checklist in the BECA Toolkit in Appendix I. The checklist will be helpful in keeping you organized and on track as you progress through the method.

Communication and Program Participation

The invitation to participate in the interview process should not be the first-time employees hear about the initiative. I would caution against this method as it does not improve employee satisfaction and engagement, just the opposite. Employees will have questions about the initiative and, to ensure inclusion and engagement, should have the opportunity to hear about the program in a forum where they can ask questions and express their feelings.

The ideal situation is to share the initiative with employees during an all-employee meeting where executive leaders discuss and promote the initiative. An all-employee meeting is also the ideal place to discuss the interview selection process. It is best to calm the potential fear that may surround the receipt of the invitation.

All employee communication should come from the Chief Executive Officer or the company's top leader to demonstrate top-of-the-house commitment to the initiative. The communication should include the who, what, when, where, why and how of the program and the method should promote and encourage employee input and questions.

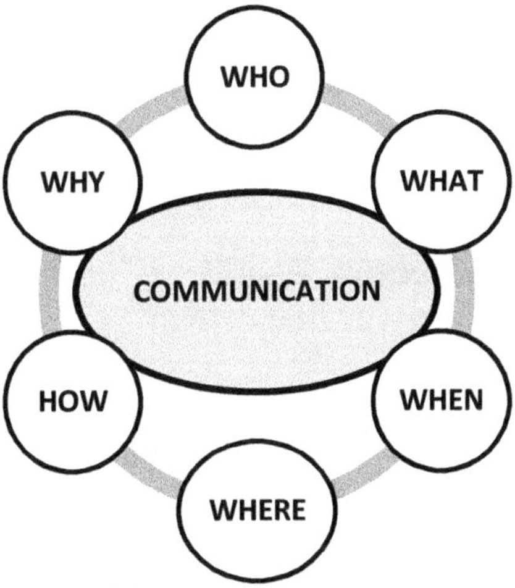

Figure 5.3 Communication components

Be sure to communicate the goals and benefits of the process and get employees excited about the great things you are doing to create a better workplace. For your convenience, sample communication templates are located in Appendix I.

Interview Methods

The interview methodology used in the BECA Method includes three groups: all executive/senior leaders and a random sample of middle managers and employees. While all senior leaders are included in the interviews, the method suggests interviewing a sample of middle managers and employees. Depending on the size of the organization, it may be unrealistic to interview the entire organization using the BECA Method, however, using a random sample has been proven to yield extraordinary results that can be generalized to the entire employee population in your company.

While testing the method for reliability and validity, I used random samples to ensure inclusion from every department within the organization. Random sampling is used to reduce bias and is a fair and simple technique to use to determine who will be included in the interviews. The only caution is that you must communicate your method to the entire organization so that employees not included in the interview portion of the method understand the process and the methods used to choose participants.

Random Sampling: How to Choose Interviewees

The first step in choosing a random sample is determining your sample size, that is, how many people you need to include in the interview process so that the results can be generalized to the entire population within your organization. This process ensures that the probability of the information you receive is highly generalizable. Everyone in the organization should be included in the list of employees to ensure that everyone has the same chance of being chosen for the interviews. There are free sample size calculators on the internet. A user-friendly, step-by-step calculator by Raosoft® that I've used many times can be found online at *http://www.raosoft.com/samplesize.html*.

To determine a random sample, let's use a simple example of an organization that has 1,000 employees and 10 departments. Using the Raosoft® online calculator, 278 employees would need to be interviewed to ensure generalizable results. Once you determine the number of people to include in the interviews, I would suggest separating your employee list by department to ensure all departments are represented.

I have found that the most efficient way to interview employees is in groups of 10-15 at each session in addition to you and a notetaker. The notetaker should be an EE practitioner or at the very least have some experience in employee engagement and be able to capture poignant information about work experiences from interviewees. Using notetakers with little to no experience could prove disastrous! How are they to know what information is pertinent? I have been there and done that!

A simple way to randomly select employees is by using an easy counting system. For example, you have 1,000 employees and 10 departments. The sample size calculation informs us that we need 278 participants. Divide the number of employees you need (278) by the number of departments (10). That gives us approximately 27 employees needed from each department. Ensure that all employees and departments are included. There is no need to list the departments in any particular order.

An easy method for selection is to randomly select every *nth* employee until you have 278 employees. For example, you can choose every 5th or every 10th employee on the list until you have 278 people chosen. Table 5.1 provides an example of selecting every 5th employee.

Table 5.1
Random Sample Employee List

	Department	Employee Name	Randomly Chosen
1	Accounting	Francisco Alvin	
2		Cheryl Azle	
3		Renee Bell	
4		Vicki Clark	
5		**Joshua Neems**	x
6	Customer Service	Rodney Diaz	
7		Victor Enzino	
8		Sharon Franks	
9		Kelvin Goss	
10		**Amy Hill**	x
11	Finance	Van Izo	
12		Violet Johnson	
13		Rose King	
14		Jessica Looze	
15		**Anthony Milner**	x

Please note that the random sample method using the Raosoft® calculator resulted in a minimum of 27 people from each department. Larger departments will yield more participants and smaller departments will yield fewer participants based on the department size. The example presented in Table 5.1 is not exhaustive and is only used as an example.

Repeat this selection process with middle managers ensuring that at least one supervisor from each department is chosen to participate. It would be ideal to include all middle managers. However, if you have a large number of middle managers, the random sample method may work best. Please note that middle managers include all frontline supervisors, managers and directors – all except executive/senior leaders.

There may be times when an employee may not be available for his or her assigned interview session. I would suggest having a list of alternates. To identify alternates, follow the same method as noted above. Once you have the first set of participants identified, set that list aside. Begin the random selection process again choosing every *nth*. For example, you can choose every 10th person this time around. Use this list as your alternates. If you have no-shows for a particular session, pull from this list to ensure your interview session size contains the adequate number of participants for generalizability (i.e., 10-15 people).

Conducting Interview Sessions

After determining the participant lists using the random sample method, schedule the interviews and invite participants. At this point, executive leaders should have communicated with all employees about the initiative so everyone in the organization is aware of and expecting this step in the process. This initial communication is critical to the process, so please do not skip it.

Sending blind invitations to middle managers and employees will only negate the positive efforts for this initiative. Be sure to communicate using all of your communication vehicles to ensure everyone is aware. Consider using employee town hall meetings, online communications sites, employee portals, flyers, newsletters, one-on-one supervisor and employee meetings, billboards and flat-screen TVs.

I have been asked if it would increase efficiency to include the feedback assessment form in the invitation you send to middle managers and employees when inviting them to participate, asking them to complete it prior to the sessions. Some practitioners may think this is more efficient, but there are downsides to distributing the forms prior to the formal interview session. Risks to distributing the form prior to the session are common to human behavior – the grapevine, employee speculation and gossip.

I have found that when employees have the form in hand, they share it with others and the conversations, speculations and gossip that will inevitably follow introduces fear and negative perceptions into the process. It is more productive to distribute the form during the interview session and gather them at the end of the session to avoid the forms floating around the company without a professional's management.

Interviews for each of the three groups should be conducted separately: Employees, middle managers, and executive leaders. Conducting interviews with "like" participants reduces anxiety and encourages participation. For example, conducting and facilitating a session that includes employees and senior leaders may not yield the results you need.

There may be employees who do not feel comfortable sharing their innermost feelings and thoughts with leaders in the room and vice versa. I have found this to be true in the sessions I have conducted. Employees feel much more at ease sharing information amongst their peers, the same for leaders.

I have received the best results in organizations where I was the third-party interviewer. Even though I was internal to the organization, I was trusted as an EE practitioner because that is how I set it up with participants as you will see later in this chapter.

Executive leaders were often amazed at what their employees shared with me about the organization, processes and culture. I suggest conducting executive leader interviews first as many times I have learned of other topics and areas of interest from leaders that I used in the middle manager and employee interviews.

During your interviews with all participants, let them know that you will only share information in aggregate. Assure them that you have had the same communication with executive leaders and you are all in agreement that no individual results will be shared and that all results will be shared in aggregate. Only facilitators will view and retain individual results. I facilitate this anonymity by asking all participants to omit their names from the assessment forms. No names, only information is gathered from the forms.

This method leaves no room for errors in anonymity and confidentiality.

Anonymity and confidentiality are critical components of this method. You will find that without these reassurances you will get little to nothing. I mean you will get absolutely nothing from employees. You will have a room full of people sitting there with their heads hung low pretending to read from a nonexistent piece of paper or checking their smartphones.

Unfortunately, many employees fear retaliation from superiors if they share information that could be viewed as negative for their department and company. So, ensuring that their individual responses will not be shared will help to move the process forward and get the results you need.

Another issue that EE practitioners may experience in the interview stage is the lack of participation. Communication from the executive leader should encourage but not demand participation. However, if session participation is poor, the results could lack generalizability.

Please alert the company liaison or executive leaders immediately if you do not have full participation from those expected to attend the session. This is also the time where your list of alternates will save the day. It is critical to impress upon employees and leaders the importance of participation to ensure that the results represent all employee thoughts, feelings and desires.

Senior Leaders

All executive leaders should be invited and strongly encouraged to participate. If a leader cannot attend, send them the form with a date for submitting it back to you. This has worked well in instances where a leader absolutely could not attend the session. Use the Executive Leader Feedback Form located in the BECA Toolkit in Appendix I to gather information from this group. A sample of the first page of the form is shown in Table 5.2.

Begin the session by ensuring that all leaders know the rationale and goals for the initiative. Also, communicate the benefits of participation and how their support and promotion of the process are critical to success. Once you have discussed the process and next steps, ask the leaders if there is any other information they would like to gather that is not already included in the interview process. Add this information to the Summary and Insight Form (Table 5.3) that you will use with employees and middle managers.

Table 5.2
Executive/Leader Feedback Form

The BECA Method **Employee Experience Feedback Form** *Executives/Senior Leaders*	
This form covers five areas that have an impact on your satisfaction and happiness with your job and workplace. Please read each statement and choose your level of agreement or disagreement using the rating scale below.	
1 – Strongly Disagree *2 – Disagree* *3 – Neither Agree nor Disagree*	*4 – Agree* *5 – Strongly Agree*
LEADERSHIP	**RATING**
1. Our workforce knows our mission (what we are trying to accomplish).	
2. Our workforce knows our vision (where we are trying to go in the future).	
3. We use the organization's values guide and direct employees.	
4. We consistently communicate important information about the organization to employees (i.e., organization's progress, direction, financials, etc.).	
5. There are methods in place that solicit employee feedback, ideas, and suggestions.	

Ask all leaders to complete the Executive Leader Assessment Form. If there are leaders that are absent from the initial meeting, coordinate the completion of their form(s) with their leaders. It is critical that all leaders participate to ensure a generalizable gap analysis. Once the leaders have completed the form, use the Summary and Insights Form (Table 5.3) to facilitate discussion about each section contained in the Executive Leader Feedback Form (i.e., leadership, growth and career progression, etc.).

Your notetaker should use the Summary and Insights form during the sessions to capture discussion details. At the end of your sessions, you should have a form already organized by category, which can prove to be extremely helpful and efficient.

I have found that the facilitated discussion yields rich information that supports and confirms the results from the feedback assessment forms. You will find that the information you are able to collect using this qualitative method can be extremely helpful when you share the results with the senior leadership team during the recap session at the end of the process. Senior leaders will have questions about the results from the quantitative results, and having additional information gathered during the facilitated discussions that confirm and adds substance, will prove invaluable.

Table 5.3
Summary and Insights Notetaking Form

The BECA Method **Summary and Insights Notetaking Form** *Comments and Themes by Category*		
LEADERSHIP [Insert Overall Score]		
Executives [Score]	**Mid-Management [Score]**	**Employees [Score]**
• Insert Notes	• Insert Notes	• Insert Notes
• Insert Notes	• Insert Notes	• Insert Notes
CUSTOMER/PATIENT FOCUS [Insert Overall Score]		
Executives [Score]	**Mid-Management [Score]**	**Employees [Score]**
• Insert Notes	• Insert Notes	• Insert Notes
• Insert Notes	• Insert Notes	• Insert Notes
QUALITY, WORK PROCESSES, CONTINUOUS IMPROVEMENT [Insert Overall Score]		
Executives [Score]	**Mid-Management [Score]**	**Employees [Score]**
• Insert Notes	• Insert Notes	• Insert Notes
• Insert Notes	• Insert Notes	• Insert Notes
GROWTH/CAREER PROGRESSION [Insert Overall Score]		
Executives [Score]	**Mid-Management [Score]**	**Employees [Score]**
• Insert Notes	• Insert Notes	• Insert Notes
• Insert Notes	• Insert Notes	• Insert Notes
REWARDS/RECOGNITION [Insert Overall Score]		
Executives [Score]	**Mid-Management [Score]**	**Employees [Score]**
• Insert Notes	• Insert Notes	• Insert Notes
• Insert Notes	• Insert Notes	• Insert Notes

Middle Managers

The number of middle management participants will vary based on the size of your company and the number of middle managers. Middle managers include all leaders below the executive/senior manager level. This includes frontline supervisors, managers, directors, senior directors, etc. Use the random sample selection method explained in the previous section to choose middle managers.

To ensure a generalizable gap analysis, ensure that at least one middle manager from each department is chosen to participate. It would be ideal to include all middle managers.

However, if you have a large number of middle managers, including all middle managers in the interview sessions may not be feasible. If this is the case, the random sample method may work best. Use the Middle Management Feedback Form located in the BECA Toolkit in Appendix I to gather information from this group. See the example in Table 5.4.

Removing employees from their jobs for the sessions may produce anxiety for leaders, especially in companies where productivity is at the forefront of the company's business scorecards. By now, leaders should be onboard and have allotted the time. I suggest no less than two hours per session.

Table 5.4
Middle Management Feedback Form

The BECA Method **Employee Experience Feedback Form** *Middle Management*		
This form covers five areas that have an impact on your satisfaction and happiness with your job and workplace. Please read each statement and choose your level of agreement or disagreement using the rating scale below.		
1 – Strongly Disagree *2 – Disagree* *3 – Neither Agree nor Disagree*	*4 – Agree* *5 – Strongly Agree*	
LEADERSHIP		**RATING**
1. I know the organization's mission (what we are trying to accomplish).		
2. I know the organization's vision (where we are trying to go in the future).		
3. Our leaders use the organization's values to provide us with direction and guidance.		
4. Our leaders consistently communicate important information about the organization to employees (i.e., organization's progress, direction, finances, etc.).		
5. There are methods in place to solicit my feedback, ideas, and suggestions.		

I have found that anything under two hours rushes the process and limits the collection of useful information and data. The group size should be 10-15 participants.

The first step with middle managers, as with all other groups, is to ensure them of anonymity and confidentiality. Get them to agree to confidentiality amongst themselves also. Let them know that what is said in the room stays in the room and that any information the facilitator deems critical to the process will be shared in aggregate. This is how the EE practitioner instills trust in the group and for the practitioner.

When they finish, use the Summary and Insights Form (Table 5.3) to facilitate a conversation about each section of the feedback form. I would suggest that you use a notetaker during this part of the session so that you, the EE practitioner, can facilitate and guide the conversation.

Middle managers can be the most challenging group from which to obtain information. It can be extremely difficult to get them to trust you and the process. I understand the behavior because I have been in their shoes. Being a middle manager is a precarious place in which to be.

Middle managers are often tasked with creating great work environments and meeting productivity goals. Employees and their superiors lean on them to make engagement and productivity happen. And when engagement and productivity do not meet expectations, middle managers are the first blamed.

Many middle managers feel that they will be blamed for any gaps in engagement and productivity, so obtaining usable information from them can be challenging. However, it is our jobs as EE practitioners to assure them that you are there to help them be successful, not point fingers. Remind them of how results will be aggregated and reported. If you are able to get this group to share amongst themselves, you will find that you can increase the bond they have to each other, which can improve their engagement.

Employees

Interacting with and interviewing front-line employees is my passion and I have gained an enormous amount of joy and satisfaction from hearing their thoughts, feelings and desires. People just want to be heard and they want to know that someone cares about them and their work situations. It is that simple.

The most important tip I can give to anyone having the pleasure of engaging with employees is to be authentic. To be effective, you must have the passion and commitment to employee engagement, and it must be real. If you do not, employees will know it and you will feel the cool breeze you get from them.

I am often asked how I am able to gain the quantity and quality of information and knowledge from my interactions with employees using the BECA Method. I have been able to uncover a multitude of issues and root causes that employees readily share with me, that eluded leaders and consulting firms. For me, it comes easy because I genuinely care about the happiness of people at work and my empathy is evident.

It is not just a job for me, it's a passion and employees can sense it. I suggest that those involved in face-to-face interviews have the same passion and empathy for employees. If not, you will not obtain the types of results that make the BECA Method successful.

For those that enjoy this work but do not have the passion for interacting with employees during interview situations, assign them to data gathering, notetaking and the administrative pieces of the work. I assure you, there is a place for those who want to make a difference in employee engagement and it does not always have to be in face-to-face interactions with employees. Be sure to understand the strengths of your team and use them accordingly.

You should now have a list of employees chosen by using the random sample selection method. Invitations should have been sent from the lead executive in the company or the EE practitioner and those agreeing to participate should be on the list. Once you know who will participate, sort the group into small groups of at least 10 but no more than 15 and set up a time to meet with them. This number should allow for flowing conversation.

The interview sessions should be organized so that each meeting has a representative from each department. I have found that mixing the groups in this manner produces much more effective conversation. If you get too many people from the same team or department in one session, you may find a reluctance to share information for fear of their coworkers' judgment and leaked conversations.

The power of the office grapevine is strong and travels quickly. People tend to share more when they are grouped with people from teams outside of their own. Be sure to let the group know that their information, as well as the conversation held in the room, is confidential. Get them to also agree to confidentiality amongst themselves. Let them know that what is said in the room stays in the room and that any information the facilitator deems critical to the process will only be shared in aggregate.

Removing employees from their jobs for the sessions often produces anxiety for leaders, especially in companies where productivity is at the forefront of the company's business scorecards. By now, leaders are onboard and they have allotted the time. I suggest no less than two hours per session. I have found that anything under two hours rushes the process and limits the collection of useful information.

Use the Employee Feedback Form (Table 5.5) to gather the data. When finished, use the Summary and Insights Form (Table 5.3) to facilitate conversation about each section. I would suggest that you use a notetaker during this part of the session so that you, the EE practitioner, can guide the conversation and flow of the session. All forms are located in Appendix I and can also be ordered by contacting the author at *TheBecaMethod@gmail.com*.

Table 5.5
Employee Feedback Form

The BECA Method **Employee Experience Feedback Form** *Employees*	
This form covers five areas that have an impact on your satisfaction and happiness with your job and workplace. Please read each statement and choose your level of agreement or disagreement using the rating scale below.	
1 – Strongly Disagree *2 – Disagree* *3 – Neither Agree nor Disagree*	*4 – Agree* *5 – Strongly Agree*
LEADERSHIP	**RATING**
1. I know the organization's mission (what we are trying to accomplish).	
2. I know the organization's vision (where we are trying to go in the future).	
3. Our leaders use the organization's values to provide us with direction and guidance.	
4. Our leaders consistently communicate important information about the organization to employees (i.e., organization's progress, direction, finances, etc.).	
5. There are methods in place to solicit my feedback, ideas, and suggestions.	

Inputting Data from the Interview Sessions

Now that you have gathered information from executive leaders, middle managers and employees, you now have a wealth of information at your fingertips. The task now is to organize the data so that you can begin to uncover the company's story and the gaps in engagement perception and expectations.

You may be pleasantly surprised to learn that the BECA Method uses simple statistics for analyzing the data. The goal is to make the BECA Method accessible, simple and cost- effective for EE practitioners. No degree in statistics needed!

The use of overly complicated statistics has just been another way to validate the need for high priced statisticians and survey firms. I have come across many people who fear or hate working with statistics. I get it! And, that is why I have made data input and analyzation for the BECA Method simple. I dare you to try it both ways, using statisticians and using the BECA Method. I guarantee you will get the same or similar, and in some cases, better root cause results.

The Data Input Form (Table 5.6) is organized into three Excel worksheets: Leaders, Middle Managers and Employees. Input the result for each group into the appropriate section(s). A detailed example of the form is located in the BECA Toolkit in Appendix I.

Table 5.6
Data Input Form

Category	EMP 1	EMP 2	EMP 3	EMP 4	TOTAL
Leadership					
Question 1	1	2	5	4	**12**
Question 2	2	5	5	3	**15**
Question 3	5	4	3	2	**14**
Question 4	5	5	5	5	**20**

Excel Worksheets →	Leaders	Mid-Mgmt.	Emp.

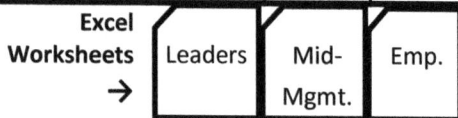

Proceed with caution as you don't want to mix these up and jeopardize ruining your results. Please note that you will need to add or remove the number of participants based on the size of your sample population. Setting up the spreadsheet may take a bit of time but once you have it done, you will reap the benefits of efficiency and you will never have to set it up again. Your spreadsheet can be used repeatedly.

Inputting this data can be a tedious task, so for this activity, use the team member who enjoys this type of work. Use the strengths of each team member for the task at which they are best. If a person is great at face-to-face interactions and communicating, I may not task them with inputting data. If you do, be sure to close all of the open windows in the office so they do not jump!

Some people find the creation of Excel spreadsheets overwhelming. If you are among them, you can request an electronic spreadsheet with formulas already input into the form from the author at *TheBecaMethod@gmail.com*.

Summary and Insights Notes

Your notetaker should use the Summary and Insights Form (Table 5.3) during the interview sessions to capture details of the discussions. The way in which this form is organized by category should prove helpful when you begin to organize and synthesize the notes. At the end of your sessions, you should have a form already organized by category, which can prove to be extremely helpful and efficient.

A few questions you can ask to begin to understand the information you've gathered are shown below. Feel free to add additional questions that may be of value to your company. The answers to these questions will help you to understand the linkages to the data you gathered from the feedback forms. Record your insights into the form and share with executives during the debriefing session. Questions to drive the conversation could include some of the following.

- What are the common themes in each group (i.e., executives, middle managers, employees)?
- Any root causes identified during the session?
- What are the outliers – information uncovered that was not shared by others?
- What was learned during the session that can improve employee engagement?
- Is there any information you need to share with other teams (e.g., legal, compliance, human resources, labor

relations, employee relations) that could help improve the services they offer?

- Is there any critical information you should share immediately to negate company risk (e.g., ethics, compliance, safety, etc.)?
- Are there similarities between each of the groups? What is dissimilar?
- What confirms and supports the data you gathered from the quantitative part of the interviews?
- Are there any conflicts between what you collected from the quantitative forms and the discussion sessions?

Developing the Gap Analysis

The gap analysis is the most insightful piece of the process because it reveals the gaps in employee engagement perceptions and expectations between executives, middle managers and employees. It is pure gold! The gap analysis can be a powerful piece of the puzzle and provides a roadmap for EE practitioners.

The gap analysis provides insight around the differences in perception and expectations between each group and how far apart or similar they are in their thoughts around engagement and culture. Using the BECA Method provides a clear and methodical process for diagnosing gaps in employee engagement that encompasses the employment hierarchy.

Oftentimes, methods used by consulting firms focus on employees and neglect to include middle managers and executives. This is a mistake and methods that take only employees into account miss important pieces of the puzzle and the resulting information and results are incomplete.

The Gap Analysis Form consists of three sections.

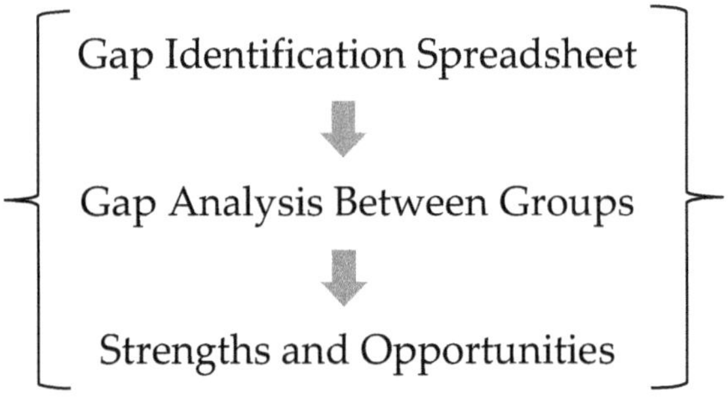

Figure 5.4. The Gap Analysis Form - Components

Pages 2 and 3 of the Gap Analysis Form houses the results from the feedback forms from executive leaders, middle managers and employees by each category of the assessment form (i.e., leadership, quality, etc.). You will need to complete this section before you can insert the final results into the gap analysis section on Page 1.

Transfer the data from the Data Input Form into the Gap Analysis Spreadsheet's Pages 2 and 3 (See Table 5.7). Be sure to transfer data into the correct spot for each group. When you have completed the data input, you will begin to see the gaps between each group. This is where the fun begins.

You should now see the differences in perceptions between each group for each category and how close or far apart the gaps between groups are for the company. Focusing on one to three opportunities may result in improvement.

Table 5.7 shows an example of the results of a completed worksheet. Note the three figures located at the bottom of each section on the form, the totals. These figures show the cumulative results for each group. These are the figures you will use to determine gaps. The Gap Analysis Spreadsheet template is located in the BECA Toolkit in Appendix I.

Table 5.7
Gap Analysis Spreadsheet

The BECA Method			
Gaps between each area assessed are detailed below. Areas scoring ≥70% are strengths. Areas scoring <70% should receive immediate focus.			
L = Leadership M = Middle Management E = Employees			
CATEGORY	Scores		
LEADERSHIP	**L**	**M**	**E**
1. Employees know the organization's mission (what we are trying to accomplish).	70	80	75
2. Employees know the organization's vision (where we are trying to go in the future).	70	80	75
3. Our leaders use the organization's values to guide and direct employees.	70	80	75
4. Our leaders consistently communicate important information about the organization to employees (i.e., organization's progress, direction, finances).	70	80	75
5. There are methods in place to solicit employee feedback, ideas, and suggestions.	70	80	75
6. When planning for the future, employees are included in the process.	70	80	75
7. Employees understand how their work contributes to the organization's plans, goals, and strategies.	70	80	75
8. Our leaders act with integrity and high ethical standards.	70	80	75
9. We have a process in place to address employee concerns that work.	70	80	75
10. Our leaders are dedicated to the fair and equal treatment of every employee.	70	80	75
11. Leaders value the inclusion and ideas of people from all backgrounds.	70	80	75
12. Senior Leaders are visible to employees.	70	80	75
LEADERSHIP FOCUS TOTAL	**70**	**80**	**75**

To obtain scores for each section of the Gap Analysis Spreadsheet, determine the difference between each group. For example, if the Leadership section score for executives is 70% and the score for Mid-Management is 75%, the result is -5 for the Executive~Mid-Management section.

This number represents the fact that executives and leaders scored the category less favorably than middle managers. We will use round figures for the examples. Repeat the same calculation for the differences between executives and employees and mid-managers and employees. An example of each category is shown in Table 5.7. Insert these results into the Gap Analysis section on the first page (Table 5.8)

In Table 5.9, please note the circle around the largest gap in perception between middle management and employees. Based on the responses to the feedback assessments, this is where the breakdown and gaps are most prevalent – between middle management and employees.

There is a minimal gap in perception between employees and executives indicating that these two groups may be in alignment with what they hold to be true. There also appears to be a minimal gap in perception between executives and middle managers. In this example, the focus should be on the relationship between middle managers and employees.

Table 5.8
Gap Analysis Form
Section 1, Page 1

The BECA Method **EMPLOYEE EXPERIENCE GAP ANALYSIS RESULTS**			
The Gap Analysis Form determines gaps in perceptions and expectations for five core areas that affect employee engagement and experience. The largest gaps exist between **[INSERT GAP INFO HERE].** Opportunities exist to improve perceptions on each category as shown below.			
GAP ANALYSIS			
CATEGORY	**Execs. ~ Mid-Mgmt.**	**Execs. ~ Employees**	**Mid-Mgmt. ~ Employees**
	Gap (-5)	**Gap (4)**	**Gap (9)**
Leadership	-10	-5	5
Customer/Patient Focus	25	15	-10
Quality, Work Processes, Continuous Improvement	-15	0	15
Growth/Career Progression	-10	5	15
Rewards, Recognition	-15	5	20
TOTAL AVERAGE SCORE	**-5**	**4**	**9**

Table 5.9
Gap Analysis Form Gap Example
Section 1, Page 1

The BECA Method **EMPLOYEE EXPERIENCE GAP ANALYSIS RESULTS**			
The Gap Analysis Form determines gaps in perceptions and expectations for five core areas that affect employee engagement and experience. The largest gaps exist between **[INSERT GAP INFO HERE].** Opportunities exist to improve perceptions on each category as shown below.			
GAP ANALYSIS			***Largest Gap*** ↓
CATEGORY	**Execs. ~ Mid-Mgmt.**	**Execs. ~ Employees**	**Mid-Mgmt. ~ Employees**
	Gap (-5)	**Gap (4)**	**Gap (9)**
Leadership	-10	-5	5
Customer/Patient Focus	25	15	-10
Quality, Work Processes, Continuous Improvement	-15	0	15
Growth/Career Progression	-10	5	15
Rewards, Recognition	-15	5	20
TOTAL AVERAGE SCORE	**-5**	**4**	**9**

The Strengths and Opportunities section creates awareness of areas that are strong or weak for the company. Strengths are categories that scored 70% or greater. Areas for Opportunities are categories that scored 69% or less.

From the completed Pages 2 and 3 of this form, place the categories that scored 70% or better in the Strengths section for executive leaders, mid-managers and employees. An example is shown in Table 5.10.

As you will see in Table 5.10, leadership is a strength for all three groups. The black and gray text represent the gaps between each group. For example, middle managers believe rewards and recognition is a strength while employees believe it is an opportunity for improvement.

Repeat the process for scores that are 69% or less for the Opportunities section. This portion of the gap analysis informs the leadership of the specific categories for action and provides insight into categories that may be working well and need sustainment.

Areas for Immediate Attention

The next step is to record areas for discussion and immediate attention. Use the Areas for Immediate Attention Form (Table 5.11) to record and inform leaders of your thoughts about where the action planning should focus. The example contains a few examples.

Table 5.10
Gap Analysis Form Example
Section 2, Page 1

Note gaps in perceptions of strengths and opportunities for improvement by category below. As a rule of thumb, areas scoring <70% are opportunities for improvement. Areas scoring ≥70% are strengths for **[INSERT COMPANY NAME]**.

	Executives	Mid-Mgmt.	Employees
Strengths	• Leadership • Customers • Careers	• Leadership • Careers • Quality	• Leadership • Customers
Opportunities	• Quality • Recognition	• Customers	• Quality • Recognition • Careers

Table 5.11
Areas for Immediate Attention

The BECA Method

AREAS FOR IMMEDIATE ATTENTION

Opportunities for Improvement	Department	Notes
• [Insert Focus Area]	• [Insert Dept.]	• [Insert Notes]
• [Insert Focus Area]	• [Insert Dept.]	• [Insert Notes]
• [Insert Focus Area]	• [Insert Dept.]	• [Insert Notes]
• [Insert Focus Area]	• [Insert Dept.]	• [Insert Notes]

These ideas should be gathered from the gap analysis results and from key ideas on the Summary and Insights forms from each group (i.e., executives/leaders, middle managers, employees).

Sharing Results with Leaders and Stakeholders

Now that you have the gap analysis complete and you have identified areas for immediate attention, it is time to share the results with the company's executive leaders. You should have the following information available for the meeting.

- Gap analysis results
- Notes from the Summary and Insights Forms
- Areas for immediate attention
- Ideas for Next Steps
- Action plan worksheets

I suggest you begin the session with a debrief of employee and middle manager attendance including your perception of generalizability. While I have had a few incidents of poor attendance, it can happen. For example, I had a session where fewer than 15 people showed up for the session. I immediately notified my liaison and we were able to combine two sessions into one.

If fewer than expected participants participate, the results could be compromised. Once leaders are aware of participation, share the gap analysis results with them. Be sure to explain the Gap Analysis Form and the methods used to obtain the gaps in perception and expectations.

The Employee Value Proposition for Action

The next step in the BECA Method is to ensure that the employee voice is heard and included in strategy development. For example, what do people value in the workplace? What would cause them to leave?

The Employee Value Proposition (EVP) Framework is an ideal tool to use to ensure that the strategies and activities you plan to improve the employee experience are relevant and important to employees.

The employee value proposition is a discussion that you should have with leaders, middle managers and employees. It will be interesting to learn how each group believes the EVP should influence strategy. The framework should be used as a method to engage all staff in discussions that identify root causes and dive deeper into assessment results to ensure understanding of issues and concerns.

The EVP framework (Figure 5.5) identifies four areas important to employees when determining whether a job and organization is a good fit for them and the potential for them to remain with the company.

The framework is useful in considering the overall employee experience and can enhance heightened emotional and intellectual connections that an employee has for his or her job, organization, manager or coworkers that, in turn, influence him/her to apply additional discretionary effort to his or her work. Using the EVP encourages leaders to consider the factors that are important to employee work life and the overall employee experience.

How to Use the Employee Value Proposition for Action

Match your company's results to each of the quadrants listed in the EVP template below. For example, if your organization scored 69% or lower on any item within a category of the Leadership section, place this result in "Leaders (Who I Work For)" quadrant of the framework under Opportunities for Improvement.

EMPLOYEE VALUE PROPOSITION

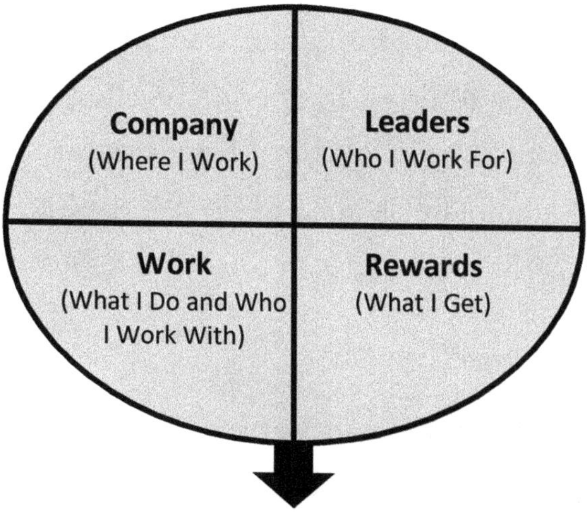

Getting It "Right Means

- Increased Engagement
- Better Work Performance
- Lower Turnover
- Better Employee and Employer Partnerships

Figure 5.5. The Employee Value Proposition

For each quadrant in the framework, identify results from your gap analysis Strengths and Opportunities section (Table 5.12). After this exercise, you will have identified areas of strength and opportunities for improvement for your company that are important to employees. Please note that some items could fit into multiple categories. You can be as creative as you like in using the form. The EVP framework template is located in the BECA Toolkit in Appendix I. The next step is to prioritize for action.

Prioritizing Objectives

Congratulations! You have now identified several areas from the gap analysis and insights documents to address. The next step is to prioritize, which will help you identify the highest impact areas for your action plan and will point out where you should invest your time, energy, and most importantly, budget. This is a critical step to ensure that your resources (i.e., time, money and people) are focused to deliver maximum results.

Take a look at Figure 5.6 for an example. Begin placing your objectives on this chart in one of the four quadrants. When I use the chart, I find it helpful to create the chart on a large Post-It notepaper or on a large whiteboard.

Table 5.12
Employee Value Proposition Template

The BECA Method **EMPLOYEE VALUE PROPOSITION TEMPLATE**	
Quadrant 1: Company (Where I work)	
Areas of Strength • Location	***Opportunities for Improvement*** • Cafeteria
Quadrant 2: Leaders (Who I work for)	
Areas of Strength • Employee Communication	***Opportunities for Improvement*** • Leadership Development
Quadrant 3: Rewards (What I get)	
Areas of Strength • Paid Time Off	***Opportunities for Improvement*** • Improved retirement fund match
Quadrant 4: Work (What I do and who I work with)	
Areas of Strength • Teamwork	***Opportunities for Improvement*** • Customer Service Training

Then you can begin to build a picture of where each objective fit in relation to the others.

The bottom quadrants represent low impact objectives and the top quadrants represent high impact objectives. The quadrants on the left represent easier to accomplish objectives and the quadrants on the right represent more difficult objectives to accomplish. Once all of your objectives are plotted, it becomes clear where you should invest your energy and resources.

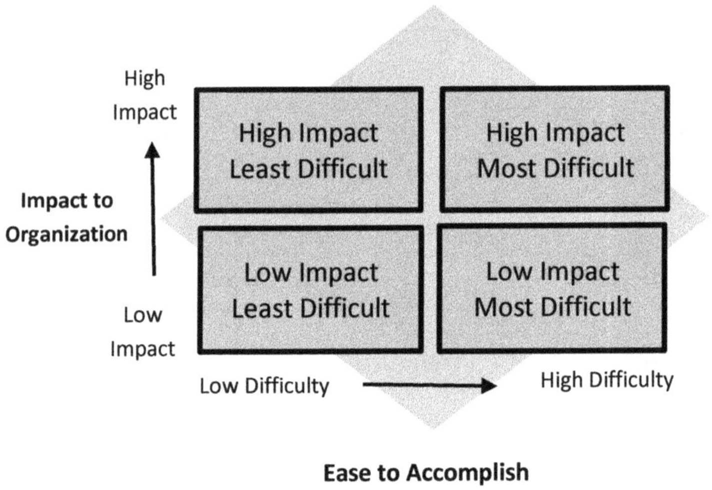

Figure 5.6. Prioritizing Objectives

You may want to begin by focusing on the "High Impact, Least Difficult" quadrant first – this is your low hanging fruit. As you begin to accomplish high impact/least difficult items, you will then most likely want to focus on your "High Impact, Most Difficult" and your "Low Impact, Least Difficult" quadrants. A Prioritization Worksheet Table is available in the BECA Toolkit in Appendix I and is shown in Table 5.13.

After you accomplish success in these quadrants, you can then turn your attention to the "Low Impact, Most Difficult" quadrant. When you finish this process, you will have an excellent visualization of which issues are most important and most achievable based on the effort needed for success.

To help you with this process, a prioritization worksheet template is located in the BECA Toolkit in Appendix I.

Table 5.13
Prioritization Worksheet

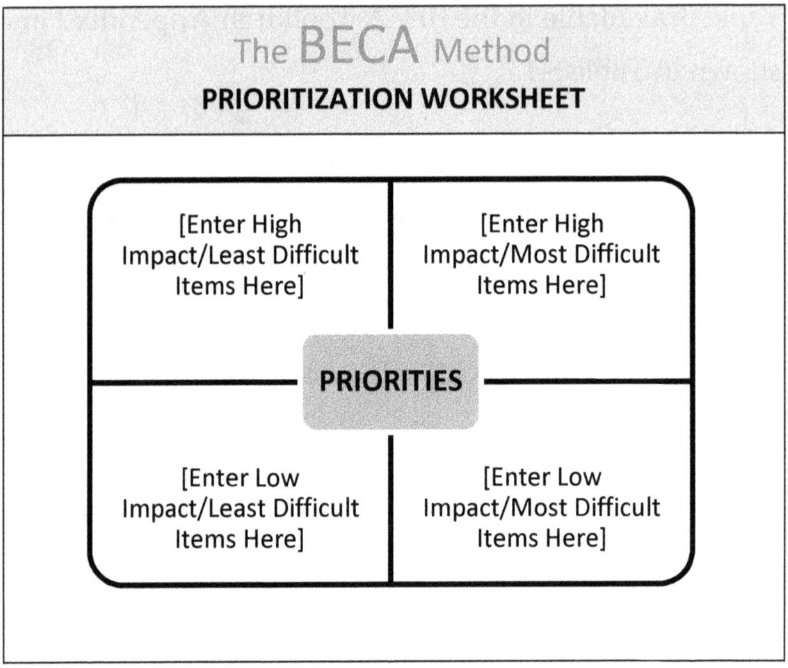

The BECA Method
PRIORITIZATION WORKSHEET
[Enter High Impact/Least Difficult Items Here]
[Enter High Impact/Most Difficult Items Here]
PRIORITIES
[Enter Low Impact/Least Difficult Items Here]
[Enter Low Impact/Most Difficult Items Here]

Begin placing your objectives on this chart in one of the four quadrants. The bottom quadrants represent low impact objectives while the top quadrants represent high impact objectives. The quadrants on the left represent easier to accomplish objectives and the quadrants on the right represent more difficult objectives to accomplish.

Action Planning

Now that you have prioritized your company's objectives, it is time to plan for action. Using the Prioritization Worksheet, record your objectives in the Action Planning Template (Table 5.14). For continuity, the template is categorized by each section on the feedback forms. You could have objectives in one, more or all of the categories depending upon what you and your leadership team chooses to focus. An example of the action plan template is shown in Table 5.14 with examples. A blank template is available in the BECA Toolkit in Appendix I.

You will note that the form includes strengths as well as opportunities for improvement. Many people strictly focus on areas of opportunities. However, it is important to spend time discussing where the organization is strong and determining plans and actions to ensure you retain those strengths. Once you complete the Action Planning Form, the next step is to identify how you will track and measure your progress and accomplishments.

Table 5.14
Employee Experience Action Planning

<table>
<tr><th colspan="4">The BECA Method

EMPLOYEE EXPERIENCE ACTION PLANNING TEMPLATE</th></tr>
<tr><td colspan="4">Use this worksheet to identify key strengths and key opportunities for improvement (OFIs). For those of high importance, establish a goal and plan of action.</td></tr>
<tr><td colspan="4">CATEGORIES</td></tr>
<tr><td colspan="4">LEADERSHIP: Develop learning development academy.</td></tr>
<tr><td>ACTION</td><td>DELIVERABLE</td><td>BY WHOM</td><td>STATUS</td></tr>
<tr><td>Create learning academy</td><td>Four Courses by March 15</td><td>A. J.</td><td>In progress</td></tr>
<tr><td colspan="4">CUSTOMER/PATIENT: Ensure customer service is embedded in processes.</td></tr>
<tr><td>ACTION</td><td>DELIVERABLE</td><td>BY WHOM</td><td>STATUS</td></tr>
<tr><td>Review processes to ensure customer service is embedded.</td><td>By Aug. 1</td><td>W.G.</td><td>In progress</td></tr>
</table>

CHAPTER 6

METRICS

"A metric is a quantifiable measure that is used to track and assess the status of a specific process or plan" (Taylor, 2017). Action plans are useless without metrics. Once you have determined your goals and strategies, how will you know when you've achieved success? How will you keep track of your progress along the way?

Metrics help you stay on target and aligned with the organization's strategies and objectives. They also ensure that individuals are held accountable for tasks and activities to which they are assigned.

Determining your goals and metrics should be based on the program initiatives you want to achieve and the impact you want to make. For example, if you decide that you want to develop a goal that influences employee retention, you would need to develop a metric that measures that goal. As an example, you determine that you want to decrease employee turnover in a specific area of your company and you develop goals, strategies and activities to influence whether people leave or stay in that area.

Your metric may look something like the example shown below in Table 6.1. The example assumes that you are measuring first-year progress. Metrics do not have to be difficult or overly statistical – even though that is what many would have you believe. Keep it simple.

Table 6.1
Sample Metric

	MEASUREMENTS					
METRIC	Baseline	Q1	Q2	Q3	Q4	Target
Team Turnover	21%	20%	20%	21%	18%	15%

Your goals and strategies should be based on the intelligence you gleaned from the gap analysis. Metrics hold us accountable to the strategies and goals we want to achieve. Without them, you will have difficulty proving your progress against goals and accomplishments.

When choosing metrics, be sure to base them on actual strategies, programs and initiatives you have documented in your action plan. Listed below are examples and types of metrics companies use to measure success.

- Financial performance
- Market share
- Reduction in turnover
- Increase in productivity
- Improvement in overall employee engagement and satisfaction results
- Satisfaction with leadership
- Culture assessment results
- EEOC complaints and grievances
- Reduced absenteeism
- Improved outcomes based on skill development as determined by needs assessments
- Customer satisfaction
- Improved safety records
- Improved outcomes (patient, sales, customer service, etc.)

- Increase in referrals
- Increase in diversity and inclusion
- Voluntary participation in company activities
- Decrease in grievances
- Decrease in unions
- Program participation (e.g., employee resource groups, company activities, town halls, etc.)

To determine metrics and measurements for your organization, based on the action plan goals you've set, you will want to ask yourself a few questions. Your responses will enable you to hone in on your needs, barriers to success and potential resources needed to accomplish goals.

Once you have answered the questions below and agreement is reached, you can begin constructing your Employee Experience Scorecard.

- What is the commitment to employee engagement in the organization?
- How many metrics will you need?
- Are the metrics realistic?
- Who will be accountable?
- Who should be involved?

- What is your organization's readiness?
- What is the budget?
- How much time should you allot to make changes and realize improvement?
- Who needs to be onboard?
- Who will sponsor or champion the program?
- What do you need to achieve program goals?
- What are the critical success factors? What must happen to be successful? Put together a list of critical success factors for each of your program goals.
- What are the barriers to success?
- How often should I measure?
- How will we evaluate and adjust?
- How will we share results and tell the employee experience story?

Metrics also serve as a communication method for creating awareness within the organization of goals and strategies planned for employee engagement improvement. If all employees are aware of the metrics and how they will be measured, the likelihood of success improves.

It is critical that your employee communication plan includes sharing the action plan and the metrics with the entire organization so that everyone feels included and knows their role in employee engagement plans and programs. A variety of communication templates are available in the BECA Toolkit located in Appendix I. Downloadable templates and forms can be requested from the author at *TheBecaMethod@gmail.com*.

CHAPTER 7

THE EMPLOYEE EXPERIENCE SCORECARD

Improve the Employee Experience and Close the Engagement Gap

In Chapter 4, I suggested that you start with a simple scorecard focusing initially on content. Focusing on what you want to achieve, your outcomes should be where you exert energy. Once you have matured in the use of the BECA Method, then move to a more sophisticated scorecard. But for now, I implore you to start simple, with a few items on the scorecard. You will thank me later.

A sample scorecard is shown in Table 7.1. Your scorecard can be as simple as this one or more elaborate. It can be whatever your company desires. However, I urge you to keep it simple so that all levels of the employee hierarchy can easily understand its content and intent.

Table 7.1
Employee Experience Scorecard

<table>
<tr><td colspan="8">The BECA Method
EMPLOYEE EXPERIENCE SCORECARD</td></tr>
<tr><td colspan="8">**MEASUREMENTS**</td></tr>
<tr><td colspan="8">**METRIC:** Reduce Turnover</td></tr>
<tr><td rowspan="2">**Current Performance**
21%</td><td colspan="4">**Progress**</td><td rowspan="2">**Target**
15%</td><td>**Result**</td><td>15%</td></tr>
<tr><td>**Q1**
20%</td><td>**Q2**
20%</td><td>**Q3**
21%</td><td>**Q4**
18%</td><td colspan="2">**Goal Accomplished**
↑Yes</td></tr>
<tr><td colspan="8">**METRIC:** Increase Diverse Talent Pool</td></tr>
<tr><td rowspan="2">**Current Performance**
2%</td><td colspan="4">**Progress**</td><td rowspan="2">**Target**
9%</td><td>**Result**</td><td>10%</td></tr>
<tr><td>**Q1**
2%</td><td>**Q2**
4%</td><td>**Q3**
4%</td><td>**Q4**
11%</td><td colspan="2">**Goal Accomplished**
↑Yes</td></tr>
<tr><td colspan="8">**To see what we're doing to improve in each area, click this link or visit [insert website here].*</td></tr>
</table>

The scorecard in Table 7.1 assumes a quarterly measurement period and assumes that the company's goal is to reduce turnover, absenteeism rates and increase the talent pool diversity. You will see that the scorecard does not include strategies and tactics. I suggest storing strategies and tactics in a separate document with a reference to that document in the footnote of the scorecard as shown at the bottom of the table.

To construct and implement your Employee Experience Scorecard, you should:

- Include items from the BECA Action Plan document.
- Align with the business's vision and strategy.
- Identify the categories that best link the business's vision and strategy and the Employee Value Proposition to its results (e.g., financial performance, company branding and reputation, employee retention, employee engagement and employee performance).
- Develop measures and meaningful standards, establishing both short-

term milestones and long-term targets.
- Ensure company-wide acceptance of the measures.
- Create budgeting, tracking, communication feedback loops, and reward systems.
- Collect and analyze performance data and compare actual results with desired performance.
- Take immediate action to close unfavorable gaps.

Congratulations! You have completed the BECA Method process. I am sure that your initial efforts were challenging. That is to be expected. I promise that as you repeat this process in your day-to-day practices, it will become easier and second nature. Most importantly, you are now equipped with a gold mine of information to inform your work as an EE practitioner, and a foundation upon which to base your work as a professional EE practitioner.

FINAL THOUGHTS

The employee experience in many U.S. companies has been neglected. While one can argue the reasons for this lack of focus, in many cases it comes down to budget and returns on investment (ROI). Unfortunately, and traditionally, the fate of employee engagement lies in the hands of the company's finance professionals – the people who determine and approve budgets, which determines programs that will move forward and gain organization and board support. To date, finance professionals have not made the leap to trusting seemingly intangible outcomes and find it challenging to link employee experience outcomes to bottom line financial gains or losses.

Finance professionals need to have tangible facts about how employee engagement programs and initiatives translate into earnings. This challenge persists. How do we as EE practitioners prove value and return on investment (ROI) when many of our outcomes are either intangible or do not qualify as cost centers (e.g., employee happiness at work, engagement, etc.)?

There are far too many generalizations and assumptions in the work of EE practitioners that are intangible. These are questions that current and future generation practitioners will need to address to move the profession forward and to gain the respect the field deserves.

During my years in this profession, the budget for employee-focused programs has been either minimal or non-existent. I fought tirelessly to prove the value of employee engagement programs and activities that employees repeatedly told us would make them happy. Year after year, employee surveys told us the same information, only to have it neglected by leaders and budget owners.

Many of us operating on shoestring budgets have had some success, but not to the level that could be accomplished if the funds were made available to "do the right things," that employees repeatedly asked for in their feedback. And as a result, many employees just stop caring and participating. Why waste their time when nothing will change was the sentiment I often heard from employees?

And then there's the "RIF Life." How do we as EE practitioners convince employees that corporate leaders care when layoffs and reductions in force continue as strategic imperatives? Is it the practitioner's responsibility to bridge this gap when layoffs and reductions in force continue to undermine the very practices we hold dear?

It is my hope that company leaders and budget owners realize the value in focusing on improving the overall employee experience, improving the workplace and valuing the people who make it happen for their companies – earning the best places to work designations.

For professionals passionate about improving the U.S. workplace and have made the choice to dedicate their careers to improving the employee experience, we must focus on proving our value, pushing for an employee engagement standard of professional practice and developing ways to show ROI. We must also convince leaders that RIFS are detrimental and a contradiction to employee engagement and financial success.

APPENDIX 1

The BECA Method

TOOLKIT

The BECA Toolkit contains all of the forms and templates you need to begin assessing and exploring the thoughts, feelings and desires of your employees and leaders, as well as gaps in engagement, as it relates to their work environment, workplace experiences and organizational culture. A list of the forms and templates is shown below along with the use for each. To obtain electronic, downloadable copies of any and all forms, please contact the author at *TheBecaMethod@gmail.com*.

TOOLKIT COMPONENTS

FORM	*USE*
The BECA Method *Checklist*	Use to organize your tasks while using the method to ensure continuity.
Employee Experience Feedback Form	Assess employee thoughts, feelings and desires around employee engagement and organizational culture.
Middle Management Feedback Form	Assess middle managements' thoughts, feelings and desires around employee engagement and organizational culture.
Executive Leader Feedback Form	Assess leaders' thoughts, feelings and desires around employee engagement and organizational culture.
Data Input Form Example	Use to input scores from each of the forms listed above: employee, middle management and leaders.
Gap Analysis Form	Use to record the cumulative scores from the Data Input Form, determining gaps in perception, expectations and thought between employees, middle managers and leaders.

Summary and Insights Feedback Form (Notetaking form)	Use to record insightful conversation from interviews with employees, middle management and leaders.
Areas for Immediate Attention Template	Use to record areas for immediate attention gained from the Gap Analysis and Summary and Insights forms. This is shared with leaders and stakeholders.
Employee Value Proposition Template	Use to develop insights into what is most important to employees and leaders.
Prioritization Worksheet	Use to help team prioritize initiatives and strategies for action.
Action Planning Template	Use to record and monitor the progress of tactics, strategies and program goals.
Employee Experience Scorecard Template	Use this form to document and track your progress and program success.
Communication Templates	Use to communicate with staff about program goals and processes.

Page 2

For electronic copies of forms and communication templates, please contact Dr. Bates at *TheBecaMethod@gmail.com.*

The BECA Method

CHECKLIST

TO DO	HOW	STATUS
DETERMINE SAMPLE SIZE	Use online sample size calculators (e.g., Raosoft®)	☐
DETERMINE INTERVIEW POPULATION	Use department data to randomly choose interview participants.	☐
SCHEDULE INTERVIEWS	Use communication templates to share the five Ws. Who, What, When, Where, Why and How.	☐
GATHER AND ANALYZE DATA	BECA Forms • Employee Feedback Form • Middle Management Feedback Form • Executive Leader Feedback Form	☐

	• Summary and Insights Feedback Form (Notes) • Data Input Form	
DETERMINE GAP ANALYSIS	BECA Forms • Data Input Form • Gap Analysis & Results Form • Summary & Insights Form • Areas for Immediate Attention	☐
DETERMINE ACTION	BECA Forms • Employee Value Proposition Form • Prioritizing Form • Action Planning Form	☐
DEVELOP EMPLOYEE ENGAGEMENT/EXPERIENCE SCORECARD	BECA Form • The Employee Experience Scorecard	☐

Page 2

**For electronic copies of forms and templates, please contact Dr. Bates at TheBecaMethod@gmail.com.*

The BECA Method

Employee Experience Feedback Form

Employees

This form covers five areas that have an impact on your satisfaction and happiness with your job and workplace. Please read each statement and choose your level of agreement or disagreement using the rating scale below.

1 – Strongly Disagree *2 – Disagree* *3 – Neither Agree nor Disagree*	*4 – Agree* *5 – Strongly Agree*

LEADERSHIP	**RATING**
1. I know the organization's mission (what we are trying to accomplish).	
2. I know the organization's vision (where we are trying to go in the future).	
3. Our leaders use the organization's values to provide us with direction and guidance.	
4. Our leaders consistently communicate important information about the organization to employees (i.e., progress, direction, finances, etc.).	
5. There are methods in place to solicit my feedback, ideas, and suggestions.	
6. When planning for the future, our leaders include us in the process.	
7. I understand how my work contributes to the organization's plans, goals, and strategies.	
8. Our leaders act with integrity and high ethical standards.	
9. There is a process in place to address employee concerns that work.	
10. Our leader(s) are dedicated to the fair and equal treatment of every employee.	
11. Our leader(s) value the inclusion and ideas of people from all backgrounds.	
12. Senior Leaders are visible to us.	
LEADERSHIP FOCUS TOTAL	

Page 1

CUSTOMER/PATIENT FOCUS	
1. I know how customer/patient satisfaction is determined at my company.	
2. I know the process for solving customer/patient problems/concerns.	
3. I am given the autonomy to solve customer/patient problems.	
4. I know how the quality of customer/patient care and service is measured at my company.	
5. Leaders (includes your supervisor and senior leaders) are transparent in sharing results and outcomes with us? (e.g., successes, research, financials, etc.).	
CUSTOMER/PATIENT FOCUS TOTAL	
QUALITY/WORK PROCESSES/ CONTINUOUS IMPROVEMENT	
1. I know how quality is measured in my work.	
2. I know how my work fits into the organization's overall measures for improvement.	
3. There is a process in place to alert my leaders when I need information and resources to effectively do my job.	
4. I have input into designing my work processes.	
5. I have autonomy over my work processes.	
6. I am satisfied with how my work is evaluated.	
7. My supervisor knows what I need to balance work/life.	
8. I am satisfied with my physical work environment.	
9. In my area, we work successfully as a team.	
10. I understand how staffing is done in my area.	
11. I can be innovative in my work at this company.	
QUALITY/WORK PROCESSES/CONTINUOUS IMPROVEMENT TOTAL	

Page 2

GROWTH/CAREER PROGRESSION	
1. Opportunities for learning and development are available to me at this company.	
2. Opportunities for career growth/progression are available to me.	
3. I have access to challenging work assignments.	
4. My supervisor encourages me to continue learning and growing in my career.	
GROWTH/CAREER PROGRESSION TOTAL	
REWARDS/RECOGNITION	
1. I am satisfied with the recognition and reward programs at this company (i.e., Employee of the Month, Service Awards, etc.).	
2. My supervisor makes every effort to recognize and reward me.	
3. I am satisfied with the company's benefits.	
4. Compared with other companies in this area, my pay is fair.	
5. I am aware of the value of my total rewards package (e.g., total amount of benefits, pay, wellness, etc.).	
REWARDS/RECOGNITION TOTAL	

What keeps you working for this organization?

___

___

___

What would cause you to leave this organization?

___

___

___

Page 3

The BECA Method

Employee Experience Feedback Form

Middle Management

This form covers five areas that have an impact on your satisfaction and happiness with your job and workplace. Please read each statement and choose your level of agreement or disagreement using the rating scale below.

1 – Strongly Disagree *2 – Disagree* *3 – Neither Agree nor Disagree*	*4 – Agree* *5 – Strongly Agree*

LEADERSHIP	**RATING**
1. I know the organization's mission (what we are trying to accomplish).	
2. I know the organization's vision (where we are trying to go in the future).	
3. Our leaders use the organization's values to provide us with direction and guidance.	
4. Our leaders consistently communicate important information about the organization to employees (i.e., progress, direction, finances, etc.).	
5. There are methods in place to solicit my feedback, ideas, and suggestions.	
6. When planning for the future, our leaders include us in the process.	
7. I understand how my work contributes to the organization's plans, goals, and strategies.	
8. Our leaders act with integrity and high ethical standards.	
9. There is a process in place to address employee concerns that work.	
10. Our leader(s) are dedicated to the fair and equal treatment of every employee.	
11. Our leader(s) value the inclusion and ideas of people from all backgrounds.	
12. Senior Leaders are visible to us.	
LEADERSHIP TOTAL	

Page 1

CUSTOMER/PATIENT FOCUS	
1. I know how customer/patient satisfaction is determined at my company.	
2. I know the process for solving customer/patient problems/concerns.	
3. I am given the autonomy to solve customer/patient problems.	
4. I know how the quality of customer/patient care and service is measured at my company.	
5. Leaders (includes your supervisor and senior leaders) are transparent in sharing results and outcomes with us? (e.g., successes, research, financials, etc.).	
CUSTOMER/PATIENT FOCUS TOTAL	
QUALITY/WORK PROCESSES/ CONTINUOUS IMPROVEMENT	
1. I know how quality is measured in my work.	
2. I know how my work fits into the organization's overall measures for improvement.	
3. There is a process in place to alert my leaders when I need information and resources to effectively do my job.	
4. I have input into designing my work processes.	
5. I have autonomy over my work processes.	
6. I am satisfied with how my work is evaluated.	
7. My supervisor knows what I need to balance work/life.	
8. I am satisfied with my physical work environment.	
9. In my area, we work successfully as a team.	
10. I understand how staffing is done in my area.	
11. I can be innovative in my work at this company.	
QUALITY, WORK PROCESSES, CONTINUOUS IMPROVEMENT TOTAL	

Page 2

GROWTH/CAREER PROGRESSION	
1. Opportunities for learning and development are available to me at this company.	
2. Opportunities for career growth/progression are available to me.	
3. I have access to challenging work assignments.	
4. My supervisor encourages me to continue learning and growing in my career.	
GROWTH/CAREER PROGRESSION TOTAL	
REWARDS/RECOGNITION	
1. I am satisfied with the recognition and reward programs at this company (i.e., Employee of the Month, Service Awards, etc.).	
2. My supervisor makes every effort to recognize and reward me.	
3. I am satisfied with the company's benefits.	
4. Compared with other companies in this area, my pay is fair.	
5. I am aware of the value of my total rewards package (e.g., total amount of benefits, pay, wellness, etc.).	
REWARDS/RECOGNITION TOTAL	

What keeps you working for this organization?

____

____

____

What would cause you to leave this organization?

____

____

____

Page 3

The BECA Method

Employee Experience Feedback Form

Executives/Senior Leaders

This form covers five areas that have an impact on your satisfaction and happiness with your job and workplace. Please read each statement and choose your level of agreement or disagreement using the rating scale below.

1 – Strongly Disagree *2 – Disagree* *3 – Neither Agree nor Disagree*	*4 – Agree* *5 – Strongly Agree*

LEADERSHIP	**RATING**
1. Our workforce knows our mission (what we are trying to accomplish).	
2. Our workforce knows our vision (where we are trying to go in the future).	
3. We use the organization's values guide and direct employees.	
4. We consistently communicate important information about the organization to employees (i.e., progress, direction, financials, etc.).	
5. There are methods in place that solicit employee feedback, ideas, and suggestions.	
6. When planning for the future, we include employees in the process.	
7. Employees understand how their work contributes to the organization's plans, goals, and strategies.	
8. I act with integrity and high ethical standards.	
9. We have a process in place to address employee concerns that work.	
10. I am dedicated to the fair and equal treatment of every employee.	
11. I value the inclusion and ideas of people from all backgrounds.	
12. I am visible to employees.	
LEADERSHIP TOTAL	

Page 1

CUSTOMER/PATIENT FOCUS	
1. Employees know how customer/patient satisfaction is determined at this company.	
2. Employees know the process for solving customer/patient problems/concerns.	
3. Employees are given the autonomy to solve customer/patient problems.	
4. Employees know how the quality of customer/patient care and service is measured at this company.	
5. Leaders are transparent in sharing results and outcomes with employees (e.g., customer/patient outcomes, customer/patient satisfaction, successes, research, etc.).	
CUSTOMER/PATIENT FOCUS TOTAL	
QUALITY/WORK PROCESSES/ CONTINUOUS IMPROVEMENT	
1. Employees know how quality is measured in their work.	
2. Employees know how their work fits into the organization's overall measures for improvement.	
3. There is a process in place to alert us to the need for information/resources employees need to do their jobs.	
4. Employees have input into designing their work processes.	
5. Employees have autonomy over how they do their work.	
6. Employees are satisfied with how their work is evaluated.	
7. We know what employees need to balance work/life.	
8. Employees are satisfied with their physical work environment.	
9. Employees at this company work successfully as a team.	
10. Employees understand how staffing is done in their areas.	
11. Employees can be innovative at this company.	
QUALITY, WORK PROCESSES, CONTINUOUS IMPROVEMENT TOTAL	

Page 2

GROWTH/CAREER PROGRESSION	
1. Opportunities for learning and development are available at this company.	
2. Opportunities for career growth/progression exist at this company.	
3. Employees have access to challenging work assignments.	
4. We encourage employees to continuously learn and grow in their careers.	
GROWTH/CAREER PROGRESSION TOTAL	
REWARDS/RECOGNITION	
1. Employees are satisfied with the recognition and reward programs in place at this company (e.g., Employee of the Month, Daisy, Service Awards, etc.).	
2. We make every effort to recognize and reward employees.	
3. Employees are satisfied with the company's benefit programs.	
4. When compared with compensation at other companies in this area, our employees are satisfied with their pay.	
5. Employees are aware of the value of their total rewards package? (e.g., total amount of benefits, pay, wellness, etc.?).	
REWARDS/RECOGNITION TOTAL	

What keeps you working for this organization?

___

___

___

What would cause you to leave this organization?

___

___

___

Page 3

The BECA Method

DATA INPUT FORM

An example of the Data Input Form (Excel spreadsheet) is shown below. Please feel free to create your own or contact the author at TheBecaMethod@gmail.com for a template that can be downloaded with formulas.

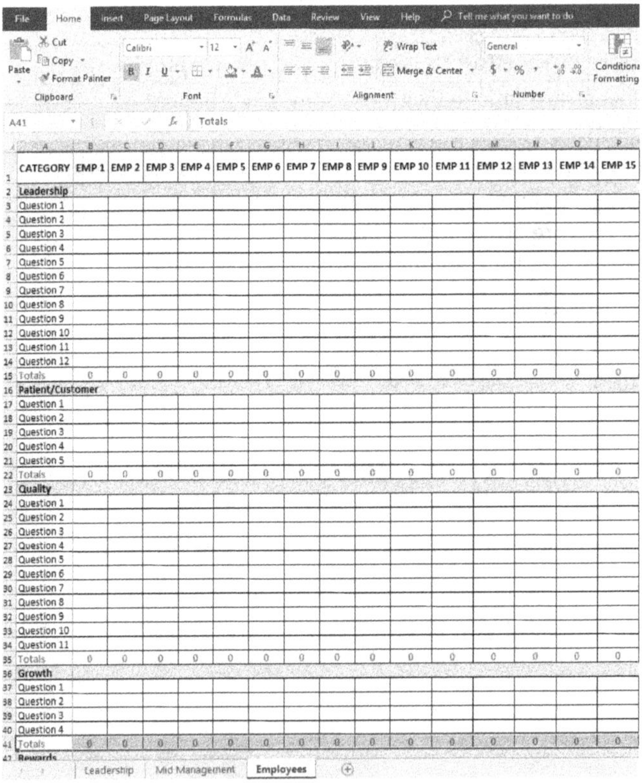

	CATEGORY	EMP 1	EMP 2	EMP 3	EMP 4	EMP 5	EMP 6	EMP 7	EMP 8	EMP 9	EMP 10	EMP 11	EMP 12	EMP 13	EMP 14	EMP 15
2	**Leadership**															
3	Question 1															
4	Question 2															
5	Question 3															
6	Question 4															
7	Question 5															
8	Question 6															
9	Question 7															
10	Question 8															
11	Question 9															
12	Question 10															
13	Question 11															
14	Question 12															
15	Totals	0	0	0	0	0	0	0	0	0	0	0	0	0	0	0
16	**Patient/Customer**															
17	Question 1															
18	Question 2															
19	Question 3															
20	Question 4															
21	Question 5															
22	Totals	0	0	0	0	0	0	0	0	0	0	0	0	0	0	0
23	**Quality**															
24	Question 1															
25	Question 2															
26	Question 3															
27	Question 4															
28	Question 5															
29	Question 6															
30	Question 7															
31	Question 8															
32	Question 9															
33	Question 10															
34	Question 11															
35	Totals	0	0	0	0	0	0	0	0	0	0	0	0	0	0	0
36	**Growth**															
37	Question 1															
38	Question 2															
39	Question 3															
40	Question 4															
41	Totals	0	0	0	0	0	0	0	0	0	0	0	0	0	0	0
42	**Rewards**															

Leadership | Mid Management | Employees

The BECA Method

EMPLOYEE EXPERIENCE GAP ANALYSIS RESULTS

The Gap Analysis Form determines gaps in perceptions and expectations for five core areas that affect employee engagement and experience. The largest gaps exist between **[INSERT GAP INFO HERE].** Opportunities exist to improve perceptions on each category as shown below.

GAP ANALYSIS

CATEGORY	Execs. ~ Mid-Mgmt.	Execs. ~ Employees	Mid-Mgmt. ~ Employees
	Gap ( )	Gap ( )	Gap ( )
Leadership			
Customer/Patient Focus			
Quality, Work Processes, Continuous Improvement			
Growth/Career Progression			
Rewards, Recognition			
TOTAL AVERAGE SCORE			

Note gaps in perceptions of strengths and opportunities for improvement by category below. As a rule of thumb, areas scoring <70% are opportunities for improvement. Areas scoring ≥70% are strengths for **[INSERT COMPANY NAME]**.

	Executives	Mid-Mgmt.	Employees
Strengths	•	•	•
	•	•	•
Opportunities	•	•	•
	•	•	•

Page 1

The BECA Method

Gap Analysis Spreadsheet

Gaps between each area assessed are detailed below. Areas scoring ≥70% are strengths. Areas scoring <70% should receive immediate focus.

L = Leadership M = Middle Management E = Employees

CATEGORY	**Scores**		
LEADERSHIP	L	**M**	**E**
1. Employees know the organization's mission (what we are trying to accomplish).			
2. Employees know the organization's vision (where we are trying to go in the future).			
3. Our leaders use the organization's values to guide and direct employees.			
4. Our leaders consistently communicate important information about the organization to employees (i.e., progress, direction, finances, etc.).			
5. There are methods in place to solicit employee feedback, ideas, and suggestions.			
6. When planning for the future, employees are included in the process.			
7. Employees understand how their work contributes to the organization's plans, goals, and strategies.			
8. Our leaders act with integrity and high ethical standards.			
9. We have a process in place to address employee concerns that work.			
10. Our leaders are dedicated to the fair and equal treatment of every employee.			
11. Leaders value the inclusion and ideas of people from all backgrounds.			
12. Senior Leaders are visible to employees.			
LEADERSHIP FOCUS TOTAL			

Page 2

	Scores		
CUSTOMER/PATIENT FOCUS	**L**	**M**	**E**
1. Employees know how customer/patient satisfaction is determined at this company.			
2. Employees know the process for solving customer/patient problems/concerns.			
3. Employees have the autonomy to solve customer/patient problems.			
4. Employees know how the quality of customer/patient care and service is measured at this company.			
5. Leaders (supervisors and senior leaders) are transparent in sharing results and outcomes with employees? (e.g., successes, research, financials, etc.).			
CUSTOMER/PATIENT FOCUS TOTAL			
QUALITY/WORK PROCESSES/CONTINUOUS IMPROVEMENT	**L**	**M**	**E**
1. Employees know how quality is measured in my work processes.			
2. Employees know how their work fits into the organization's overall measures for improvement.			
3. There is a process in place to alert leaders when employees need information and resources to effectively do their jobs.			
4. Employees have input into designing their work processes.			
5. Employees have autonomy over their work processes.			
6. Employees are satisfied with how their work is evaluated.			
7. Leaders know what employees need to balance their work/life.			

Page 3

	Scores		
8. Employees are satisfied with their physical work environments.			
9. We work successfully as a team.			
10. Employees understand how staffing is done in their areas.			
11. Employees can be innovative in my work at this company.			
QUALITY/WORK PROCESSES/CONTINUOUS IMPROVEMENT TOTAL			
GROWTH/CAREER PROGRESSION	L	M	E
1. Employees have the opportunity for learning and development.			
2. Opportunities for career growth/progression are available to employees.			
3. Employees have access to challenging work assignments.			
4. Employees are encouraged to continue learning and growing in their careers.			
GROWTH/CAREER PROGRESSION TOTAL			
REWARDS/RECOGNITION	**L**	**M**	**E**
1. Employees are satisfied with the recognition and reward programs in place at this company (e.g., Employee of the Month, Daisy, Service Awards, etc.).			
2. My supervisor makes every effort to recognize employees.			
3. Employees are satisfied with the company's benefits.			
4. Compared with other companies in this area, employees are satisfied with their pay.			
5. Employees are aware of the value of their total rewards package (e.g., total amount of benefits, comp, wellness, etc.).			
REWARDS/RECOGNITION TOTAL			

Page 4

The BECA Method

Summary and Insights Notetaking Form

Comments and Themes by Category

LEADERSHIP [Insert Overall Score]		
Executives [Score]	**Mid-Management [Score]**	**Employees [Score]**
• **Insert Notes**	• **Insert Notes**	• **Insert Notes**
• **Insert Notes**	• **Insert Notes**	• **Insert Notes**
CUSTOMER/PATIENT FOCUS [Insert Overall Score]		
Executives [Score]	**Mid-Management [Score]**	**Employees [Score]**
• **Insert Notes**	• **Insert Notes**	• **Insert Notes**
• **Insert Notes**	• **Insert Notes**	• **Insert Notes**
QUALITY, WORK PROCESSES, CONTINUOUS IMPROVEMENT [Insert Overall Score]		
Executives [Score]	**Mid-Management [Score]**	**Employees [Score]**
• **Insert Notes**	• **Insert Notes**	• **Insert Notes**
• **Insert Notes**	• **Insert Notes**	• **Insert Notes**
GROWTH/CAREER PROGRESSION [Insert Overall Score]		
Executives [Score]	**Mid-Management [Score]**	**Employees [Score]**
• **Insert Notes**	• **Insert Notes**	• **Insert Notes**
• **Insert Notes**	• **Insert Notes**	• **Insert Notes**
REWARDS/RECOGNITION [Insert Overall Score]		
Executives [Score]	**Mid-Management [Score]**	**Employees [Score]**
• **Insert Notes**	• **Insert Notes**	• **Insert Notes**
• **Insert Notes**	• **Insert Notes**	• **Insert Notes**

The BECA Method

AREAS FOR IMMEDIATE ATTENTION

Opportunities for Improvement	Department	Notes
• [Insert Focus Area]	• [Insert Dept.]	• [Insert Notes]
• [Insert Focus Area]	• [Insert Dept.]	• [Insert Notes]
• [Insert Focus Area]	• [Insert Dept.]	• [Insert Notes]
• [Insert Focus Area]	• [Insert Dept.]	• [Insert Notes]
• [Insert Focus Area]	• [Insert Dept.]	• [Insert Notes]
• [Insert Focus Area]	• [Insert Dept.]	• [Insert Notes]
• [Insert Focus Area]	• [Insert Dept.]	• [Insert Notes]
• [Insert Focus Area]	• [Insert Dept.]	• [Insert Notes]
• [Insert Focus Area]	• [Insert Dept.]	• [Insert Notes]
• [Insert Focus Area]	• [Insert Dept.]	• [Insert Notes]
• [Insert Focus Area]	• [Insert Dept.]	• [Insert Notes]
• [Insert Focus Area]	• [Insert Dept.]	• [Insert Notes]

The BECA Method **EMPLOYEE VALUE PROPOSITION TEMPLATE**	
Quadrant 1: <u>Company</u> (Where I work)	
<u>Areas of Strength</u> • [Insert Strengths] • [Insert Strengths]	***<u>Opportunities for Improvement</u>*** • [Insert Opportunities] • [Insert Opportunities]
Quadrant 2: <u>Leaders</u> (Who I work for)	
<u>Areas of Strength</u> • [Insert Strengths] • [Insert Strengths]	***<u>Opportunities for Improvement</u>*** • [Insert Opportunities] • [Insert Opportunities]
Quadrant 3: <u>Rewards</u> (What I get)	
<u>Areas of Strength</u> • [Insert Strengths] • [Insert Strengths]	***<u>Opportunities for Improvement</u>*** • [Insert Opportunities] • [Insert Opportunities]
Quadrant 4: <u>Work</u> (What I do and who I work with)	
<u>Areas of Strength</u> • [Insert Strengths] • [Insert Strengths]	***<u>Opportunities for Improvement</u>*** • [Insert Opportunities] • [Insert Opportunities]

The BECA Method

PRIORITIZATION WORKSHEET

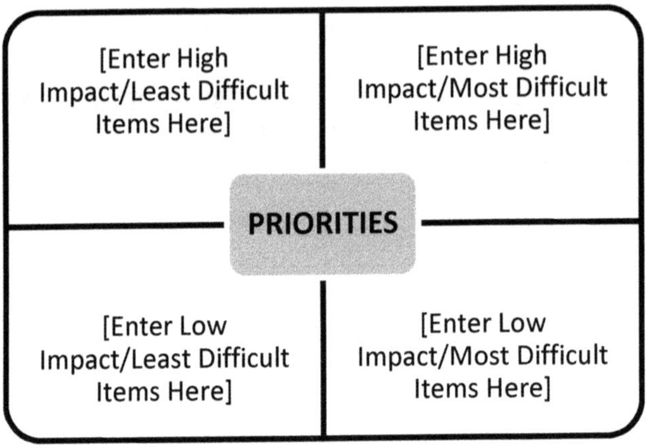

Begin placing your objectives on this chart in one of the four quadrants. The bottom quadrants represent low impact objectives while the top quadrants represent high impact objectives. The quadrants on the left represent easier to accomplish objectives and the quadrants on the right represent more difficult objectives to accomplish.

The BECA Method

EMPLOYEE EXPERIENCE ACTION PLANNING TEMPLATE

Use this worksheet to identify key strengths and key opportunities for improvement (OFIs). For those of high importance, establish a goal and a plan of action.

CATEGORIES

LEADERSHIP: [Insert goal here]

ACTION	DELIVERABLE	BY WHOM	STATUS

CUSTOMER/PATIENT: [Insert goal here]

ACTION	DELIVERABLE	BY WHOM	STATUS

QUALITY, WORK PROCESSES, CONTINUOUS IMPROVEMENT: [Insert goal here]

ACTION	DELIVERABLE	BY WHOM	STATUS

GROWTH & CAREER PROGRESSION: [Insert goal here]

ACTION	DELIVERABLE	BY WHOM	STATUS

REWARDS & RECOGNITION: [Insert goal here]

ACTION	DELIVERABLE	BY WHOM	STATUS

The BECA Method **EMPLOYEE EXPERIENCE SCORECARD**							
MEASUREMENTS							
METRIC: Reduce Turnover							
Current Performance	**Progress**				**Target**	**Result**	
	Q1	Q2	Q3	Q4		**Goal Accomplished**	
METRIC: Increase Diverse Talent Pool							
Current Performance	**Progress**				**Target**	**Result**	
	Q1	Q2	Q3	Q4		**Goal Accomplished**	
To see what we're doing to improve in each area, click this link or visit this website.** ***[insert website here]							

The BECA Method

COMMUNICATION TEMPLATES

This section contains email templates you can use to share program information, invite program participants and communicate with all employees. These templates are suggestions, a starting point, and should be created in your organization's language, tone and branding specifications.

Template 1: Program Introduction/Roll Out (All Staff)

Dear [Insert Name],

We are pleased that you choose to work at [insert company name] and we want you to continue to share your knowledge, skill and abilities with us. We know that you can choose to work elsewhere, but we don't want that. We are continuously working to earn your loyalty. Over the next few months, we are embarking on a program to learn more about why you work here and what keeps you happy, but we need your help. Soon, we will randomly choose employees to work closely with us to identify ways to keep our workplace great. If you are not chosen for the small group meetings, please rest assured that we will call on you in subsequent meetings (e.g., Town Halls) to gather your feedback and provide you with the opportunity to share your thoughts and feelings.

We are so excited to work with you to make our workplace better. If you have any questions, please reply to this email or feel free to contact [insert name] for more information.

[insert program lead name and contact information]

Template 2: Invitation to Participants (Employees and Middle Managers)

Dear [Insert Name],

Congratulations! You have been randomly chosen to participate in our organization's employee experience improvement program. We are serious about improving your work experience at [insert company name], but we need your help. Randomly, we chose [insert number of people] to represent each department in the company. This is an amazing opportunity to share your thoughts about your workplace and how we can make it better for you.

The meeting will be held [insert date] in the [insert place] conference room. Your manager has been advised and is happy for you to participate. Please note that these meetings will be confidential, so feel free to express any feelings and desires you have about your workplace during the meeting. We are happy about your participation. However, if you would like to opt out, no problem. Respond to this email letting us know and we will go from there. We do hope that we can hear your voice.

[insert program lead name and contact information]

Template 3: Thank You and Next Steps to Participants (Employees and Middle Managers)

Dear [Insert Name],

Thank you so much for your participation in the employee experience program. Your input is so valuable to us. The next steps are to cumulate and aggregate the responses and develop a report to share with leadership. Just a reminder that we will not use names in the report, only the cumulative information gathered from the interviews.

We plan to hold Town Hall Meetings in [insert month] to share the report with all employees. This meeting will give everyone the opportunity to give their feedback and input. Our goal is to gather input from staff and leaders and develop strategies for moving forward to improve our workplace. We hope that you will continue to support the program and we may call on you for specific activities as we move forward. We truly appreciate your participation and your help in making this a great place to work.

[insert program lead name and contact information]

Additional communication will need to be drafted and shared with employees once you have identified program strategies, tactics and timelines and for keeping employees informed about project progress and accomplishments.

RESOURCES

This section contains resources that may be helpful in your day-to-day work as an Employee Engagement Practitioner. The list is by no means exhaustive, but should get you started and help you in your research for trends and thought leadership in employee engagement.

- Advisory Board
  http://www.advisory.com

- Blessingwhite
  http://www.blessingwhite.com

- The Employee Engagement Group
  https://employeeengagement.com/engagement-resources/

- Engage for Success
  http://www.engageforsuccess.org

- Forbes
  http://www.forbes.com

- Fortune
  https://www.greatplacetowork.com
- Gallup
  http://www.gallup.com
- Glint
  http://www.glintinc.com
- Globoforce
  http://www.globoforce.com
- IBM
  http://www.ibm.com
- Limeade
  http://www.limeade.com
- LinkedIn
  http://www.linkedin.com
- O.C. Tanner
  http://www.octanner.com
- Modern Healthcare
  http://www.modernhealthcare.com
- Raosoft® Sample Size Calculator
  http://www.raosoft.com/samplesize.html
- Society for Human Resource Management
  http://www.shirm.com
- TINYpulse
  http://www.tinypulse.com

REFERENCES

Buckingham, M. & Coffman, C. (1999). *First, break all the rules: What the world's greatest managers do differently.* New York, NY: Simon & Shuster.

Catalyst (2016). *Turnover and retention*. Retrieved October 31, 2017 from http://www.catalyst.org/knowledge/turnover-and-retention.

Coffman, C. & Gonzalez-Molina, G. (2002). *Follow this path: How the world's greatest organizations drive growth by unleashing human potential.* New York, NY: Warner Books, Inc.

Creswell, J. (2005). *Educational research: Planning, conducting, and evaluating quantitative and qualitative research.* Upper Saddle River, NJ: Pearson Education, Inc.

Davis, N. (2017). *What is employee engagement?* Retrieved April 8 2017 from http://davisassociates.co.uk/what-is-employee-engagement/.

Gallup (2017). *State of the American workplace.* Retrieved April 9, 2017 from http://www.gallup.com/services/178514/state-american-workplace.aspx.

Gallup (2018). *State of the American workplace*. Retrieved September 6, 2018 from http://business.gilbertaz.com/events/details/state-of-the-american-workplace-presented-by-gallup-5035

Harris, D. (2016). *How often should you conduct employee engagement surveys?* Retrieved September 12, 2018 from https://www.quantumworkplace.com/future-of-work/how-often-should-you-conduct-an-employee-survey-annually-provides-better-results

Harter, J.K., Schmidt, T.L., Hayes. (2002). *Business-unit-level relationship between employee satisfaction, employee engagement, and business outcomes. A meta-analysis.* Journal of Applied Psychology, 87*(2)*, 268-269.

Little, B. & Little P. (2006). *Employee engagement: Conceptual issues*. Journal of Organizational Culture, Communications and Conflict: 10,1 ProQuest Central, p. 111.

M.I.T Human Resources (2009). *Keeping remaining employees engaged after a layoff*. Retrieved April 10, 2017 from http://hrweb.mit.edu/system/files/all/oec/toolkit/engaged_layoff_0409.pdf.

Murphy, M. (2015) *Don't expect layoff survivors to be grateful*. Retrieved April 10, 2017 from http://www.leadershipiq.com/blogs/leadershipiq/29062401-dont-expect-layoff-survivors-to-be-grateful.

Neuman, L. (2003). *Social research methods. Qualitative and quantitative approaches* (5th ed). Boston: Pearson Education, Inc.

Riordan, C (2013). *We all need friends at work*. Harvard Business Review. Retrieved October 31, 2017 from https://hbr.org/2013/07/we-all-need-friends-at-work.

Robinson D, Perryman S, Hayday S. (2004). *The drivers of employee engagement*, Report 408, Institute for Employment Studies. Retrieved August 23, 2018 from https://www.employment-studies.co.uk/report-summaries/report-summary-drivers-employee-engagement.

Taylor, J. (2017). *What is a KPI, metric or measure?* Retrieved August 27, 2018 from https://www.klipfolio.com/blog/kpi-metric-measure.

Vance, R. (2006). *Employee engagement and commitment. A guide to understanding, measuring and increasing engagement in your organization.* Society for Human Resource Management.

Uchitelle, L (2006). *The disposable American: Layoffs and their consequences.* Alfred A. Knopf. Inc.

Wellins, R., & J. Concelman. (2005). *Creating a culture of engagement.* Workforce Performance Solutions. Retrieved August 1, 2005 from www.WPSmag.com.

The BECA Method

ABOUT THE AUTHOR

Dr. Cheryl Bates holds a doctorate in Management with emphasis on Organizational Leadership. Cheryl's experience in human resource functions includes employee engagement, new hire onboarding, diversity and inclusion, employee communications, employee engagement surveys and administration, culture assessments and strategy, productive work behaviors and leadership development. An author and entrepreneur, she is the principal consultant in CRB Consulting Services and owns a real estate brokerage firm. Dr. Bates is driven by a relentless pursuit of the factors that drive happiness in the workplace and has dedicated her career to helping companies and employees understand the linkage between financial outcomes and the employee experience. Dr. Bates is a certified Helios™ (formerly Strengthscope™) practitioner and a certified teacher of English as a second language.

Contact Dr. Bates at *TheBecaMethod@gmail.com.*

www.ingramcontent.com/pod-product-compliance
Lightning Source LLC
Chambersburg PA
CBHW071852200326
41519CB00016B/4341
9780692194799